# DENDRITIC MACROMOLECULES

**Dr. Pravinkumar. M. Patel, M. Sc., Ph.D.**
Associate Professor
Industrial Chemistry Department,
V.P. & R.P.T.P. Science College affiliated to Sardar Patel University,
Vallabh Vidhyanagar, Anand, Gujarat, INDIA.

## About Author

Pravinkumar Patel is Associate Professor of Industrial Chemistry department, V.P. & R. P. T. P. Science College affiliated to Sardar Patel University, Vallabh Vidhyanagar, Gujarat, India. He was awarded Ph.D. degree in subject of Chemistry in the year 1999 from Sardar Patel University, Vallabh Vidhyanagar. His research interests include Polymer Chemistry, Synthesis of heterocyclic compounds and dendrimers of biological interests. He has published more than fifty research papers, review articles in peer reviewed national and international journals and presented several research papers based on his research group findings. He has also given invited talks on research interest in India. He has completed many Research Projects funded by University Grant Commission, New Delhi. Three students have been awarded Ph.D. degree in the subject of Chemistry under his supervision and present three students are pursuing Ph.D. degree in Industrial Chemistry subject. Many post graduates students were completed their P.G. dissertation work under the supervision of Dr. Patel. Dr. Pravinkumar Patel rendered services in starting up the Pharmaceuticals practical for the B Sc. Industrial Chemistry Vocational courses funded by UGC, Dr. Patel is member of many organizing committee for seminars and conferences, and also member of faculty of science and board of Industrial chemistry, Sardar Patel University, Vallabh vidyanagar.

# Preface

Dendrimers are novel class of polymers. Dendrimers represents fourth new class of macromolecular architectures. Similar to linear polymers, they composed of a large number of monomer units that were chemically linked together. Dendritic polymer possess several unique properties such as monodisperse molecular weight distribution, high degree of branching, nanometer size, and compact globular void spaced structures.Candidature of dendritic macromolecules have been investigated in several field of applications such as Drug delivery, Catalysis, Sensors, Drug Solubilisation and Water Remediation.

The researchers the field of chemical science and engineering, materials science and engineering, medicinal science and technology, etc. could use this book as reference for their respective profession. Chapter-1 describes, basic concepts of dendrimer chemistry which includes historical development, structure, properties and significance of dendrimer. A brief historical development led to dendrimer is provided. Dendrimer design, structural aspects are also given along with unique properties and significance.

Second Chapter describes routes of dendrimer synthesis. Traditionally "Divergent routes" and "Convergent routes" were prominent for dendrimer synthesis. With exploration, novel recently accelerated routes for dendrimer synthesis have been invented which are discussed here in.

Third chapter deals with types of dendritic architectures and their importance. Applications of dendrimer in various fields such as drug delivery, catalysis, membrane separation technology, drug solubilisation etc have been discussed.

## Table of Contents

# 1. DENDRIMER: INTRODUCTION

## 1.1 Historical Development

Polymer science is a subfield of materials science which deals with polymers, primarily synthetic polymers such as plastics and elastomers. The field of polymer science includes researchers in multiple disciplines including chemistry, physics, and engineering [1]. The earliest known work of polymer science was done in pre-Columbian Mexico.The Mesoamericans knew how to combine latex of the rubber tree with the juice of the morning glory plant in different proportions to get rubber with different properties for different products, such as bouncing balls, sandals, and rubber bands dating back to 1600 B.C. [2].The first modern example of polymer science is Henri Braconnot's work in the 1830s. Braconnot, along with Christian Schönbein and others, developed derivatives of the natural polymer cellulose, producing new, semi-synthetic materials, such as celluloid and cellulose acetate [1]. The term "polymer" was coined in 1833 by Jöns Jakob Berzelius. In the 1840s, Friedrich Ludersdorf and Nathaniel Hayward independently revealed that adding sulfur to raw natural rubber (polyisoprene) helped prevent the material from becoming sticky. In 1844 Charles Goodyear received a U.S. patent for vulcanizing natural rubber with sulfur and heat. Thomas Hancock had received a patent for the same process in the UK the year before. This process strengthened natural rubber and prevented it from melting with heat without losing flexibility. This made practical products such as waterproofed articles possible. It also facilitated practical manufacture of such rubberized materials. Vulcanized rubber represents the first commercially successful product of polymer research. In 1884 Hilaire de Chardonnet started the first artificial fiber plant based on regenerated cellulose, or viscose rayon, as a substitute for silk, but it was very flammable [1]. In

1907 Leo Baekeland invented the first synthetic polymer, a thermosetting phenol–formaldehyde resin called Bakelite [3]. Despite significant advances in polymer synthesis, the molecular nature of polymers was not understood until the work of Hermann Staudinger in 1922 [4].Hermann Staudinger was the first to propose that polymers consisted of long chains of atoms held together by covalent bonds. It took over a decade for Staudinger's work to gain wide acceptance in the scientific community, work for which he was awarded the Nobel Prize in 1953.The World War II era marked the emergence of a strong commercial polymer industry. The limited or restricted supply of natural materials such as silk and rubber necessitated the increased production of synthetic substitutes, such as nylon [5] and synthetic rubber [6]. In the intervening years, the development of advanced polymers such as Kevlar and Teflon have continued to fuel a strong and growing polymer industry.

Historically polymer science have mainly dealt with linear polymers, but since 1970s a great deal of interest was increased in highly branched macromolecules because of their unique properties which facilitate their use in "Host-Guest Chemistry" [7]. One such macromolecule was first invented by Fritz Vogtle in 1979[8]. The products were then termed as "cascade molecules". These molecules were prepared by iterative reaction sequence involving Micheal addition of acrylonitrile to an amine in first step and reduction of nitrile to amine in the second. The synthesized macromolecules were relatively small in nature but first synthetic route to dendrimer was outlined [Figure 1].

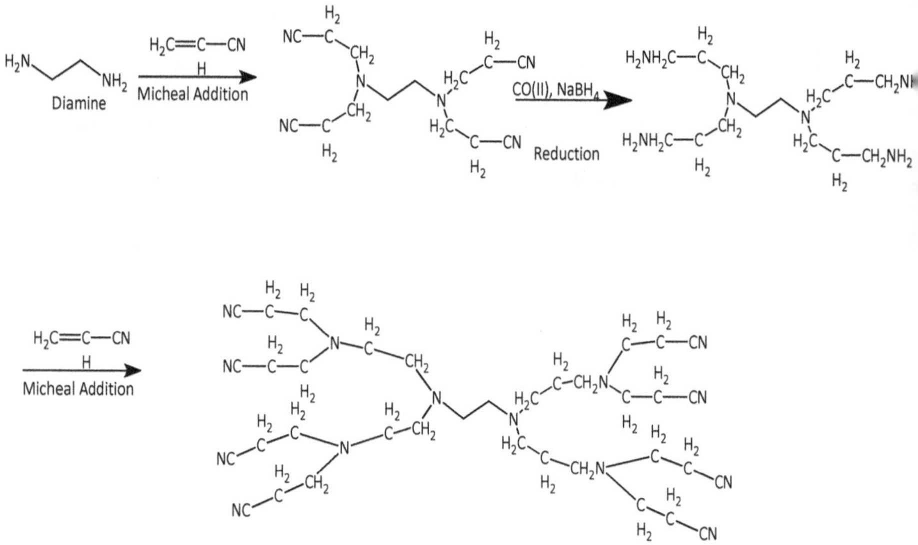

**Figure 1.** Fritz Vogtle's Synthesis of Polypropylene-imine dendrimer

Denkewalter et al. then reported synthesis of polylysine dendrimers with lysine units [Fig 2] via divergent method in three patents in early 1980s [9, 10, 11].

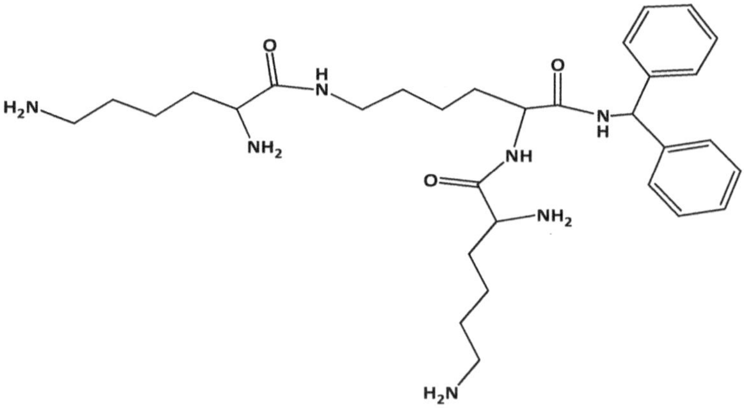

**Figure 2.** Denkewalter's Polylysine dendrimers with lysine units.

In 1983, Maciejewski developed a dense packing concept for cascade like polymer [12]. In 1983, French physicist de Gennes (Noble laureate in 1991) and Hervert presented a report on limits in growth of branched molecules due to steric hindrance at higher generation which is known as "de Gennes dense packing"[13] phenomenon or "Starburst limit"[14]. Further statistical models were also combined with the cascade theory [15] and De Gennes also termed these highly brached molecules as soft material [16].

Tomalia et al. [17] in 1985 at Dow Corporation developed polyamidoamine type macromolecules, which were termed as "Starburst dendrimer". The synthetic route was similar to that of cascade molecules i.e. it required Micheal addition of methylacrylate to an amine then followed by conversion of ester into amine by amidation with ethylene diamine. The dendrimers were synthesized up to generation 10 with decrease in purity and perfection. Tomalia described ester terminated stages as half generations and amine terminated stages as full generations [Figure 3].

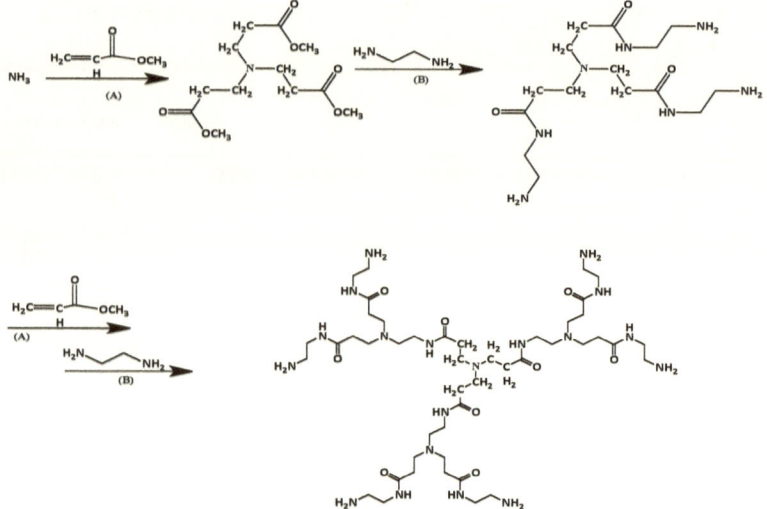

**Figure 3.** Tomalia's Synthesis of Starburst Dendrimer

Also in 1985 Newkome et al reported divergent route to water soluble, highly branched, hydroxyl terminated dendrimers denoted as "Arborols"[Figure 4][18,19].

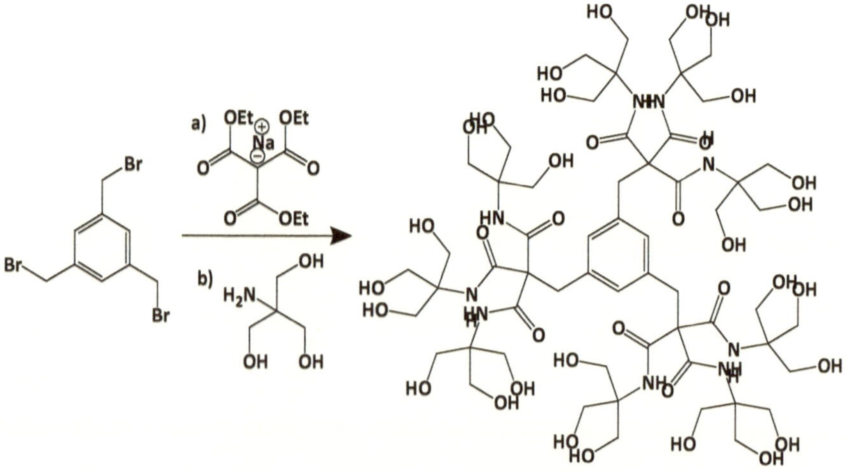

**Figure 4.** Newkome's synthesis of Arborols

In 1990, Frechet and Hawker described the first convergent synthesis of dendrimers. The poly (arylether) dendrimers were grown from outside to core [Figure 5] [20]. In the very same year Miller and Neenansynthesized the first hydrocarbondendrimers [Figure 6] based exclusively on arene units, also using a convergent synthetic strategy [21].

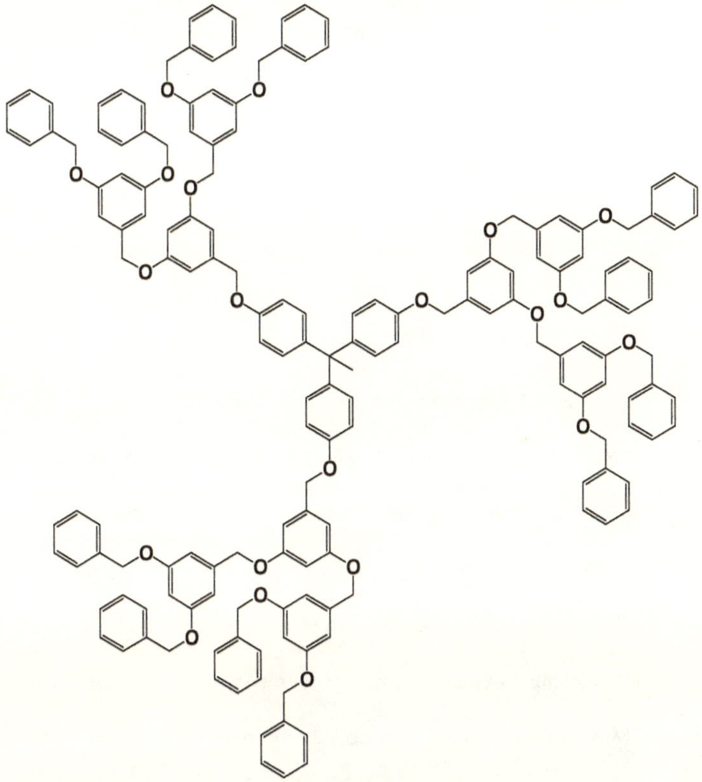

**Figure 5.** Frechet's dendrimer synthesized by Convergent Route

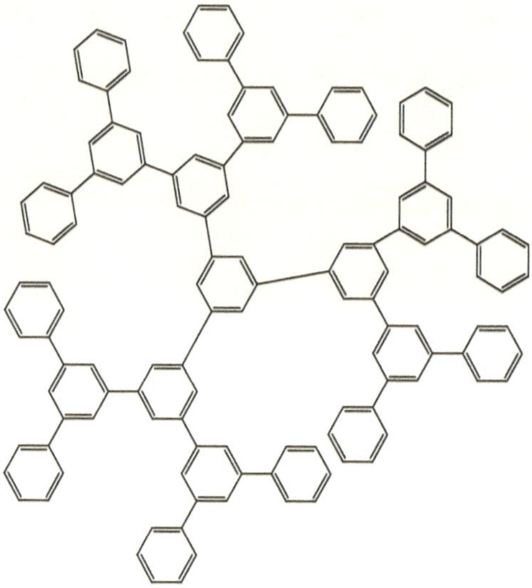

**Figure 6.** Hydrocarbon dendrimer (Miller and Neelan)

In this introduction, historical development is limited to initial developments in dendrimer chemistry. It was seen that from early 1990s, Interest in dendrimer chemistry was increased which can be manifested from number of reviews, research papers, patents and articles published in the field of dendrimer chemistry, which were numbered into 100s from 1990 to 1995. Since 1995 the number of publications in dendrimer synthesis has been increased up to 1000s per year. Most of these publications discusses different routes for dendrimer synthesis, properties and applicability in different fields ranging from medicine to sensing applications [22, 23]

## 1.2. Dendritic/ HyperbranchedMacromolecules: Fourth New Class of Polymeric Architecture

Previously there were three classes of polymeric architectures were known 1) linear polymers e.g. Nylon and Plexiglass, 2) Branched Polymers e.g. polyvinyl alcohol or polystyrene and 3) cross-linked polymers e.g. rubber and epoxy. At present dendritic topology has been emerged as fourth new class of polymeric or macromolecular architecture [24-27] [fig. 7]. Structures of polymers in dendritic topology resembles to a Tree.

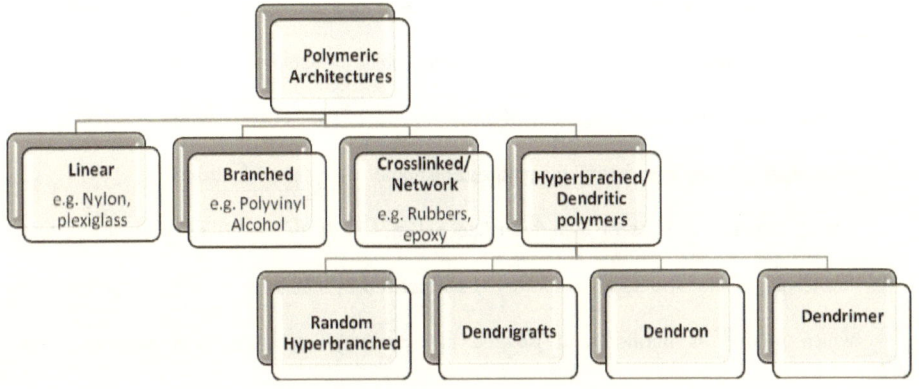

**Figure 7.** Illustrates classes of polymeric architectures.

Presently this fourth class consist of following subclasses [Figure 7] 1) Random hyperbranched polymers 2) Dendrigrafts 3) Dendron and 4) Dendrimer. *Random Hyperbranched Polymers* are produced by one pot polymerization of $AB_x$ type monomers involving polycondensation, ring opening or polyaddition reactions hence products are polydisperse and randomly branched. To enhance availability of dendritic structures,they are for some purpose used as "dendrimer mimics" because of their more facile synthesis. Dendrigrafts are most recently discovered and least understood class of dendritic polymers. The physicochemical properties of hyperbranched polymers are intermediate between dendrimers and linear polymers [28].

Dendrigrafts can also be constructed with well-defined structures like dendrimer i.e. with low monodispersity. However in contrast to dendrimers, dendrigrafts are centered on a linear polymer chain to which branches are attached. These co-polymer chains are further modified with other co-polymer chains and so, on. These are also polydisperse [29].

Dendron is termed as a dendritic wedge without a core, the dendrimer can be assembled from two or more dendrons. Dendrons are very useful tool during synthesis of dendrimer by convergent route. Dendrons, which are commercially available and applied with success in covalent and noncovalent assembly of dendrimers are "Frechet type dendrons" [20, 30, 31]. This dendrons have been useful for synthesizing numerous types of dendrimer.

Fourth member of class of hyperbranched polymer is dendrimer. Dendrimer has perfectly branched globular structure. Dendrimer is synthesized by step by step synthetic procedure in which product is purified and isolated in each step so, synthesized dendrimer have monodisperse molecular weight distribution.

## 1.3. Structure of Dendrimer

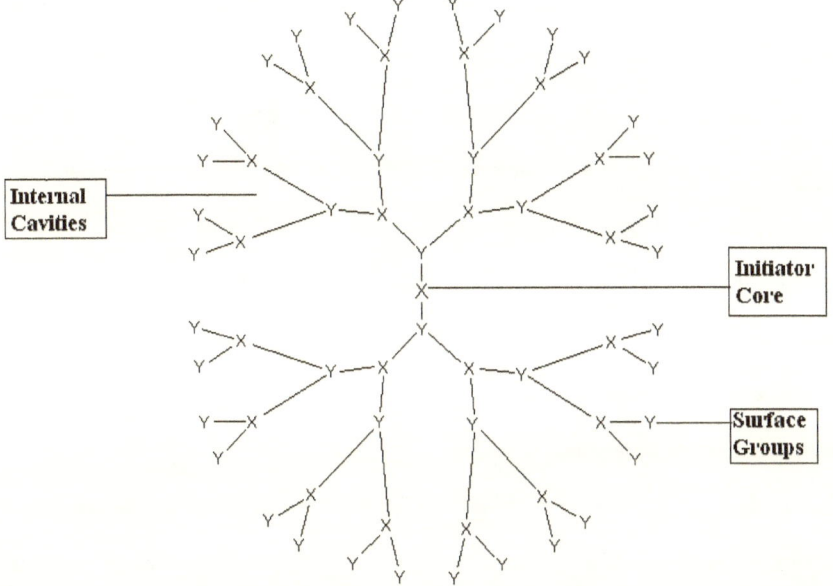

**Figure 8.** Structure of Dendrimer showing its three Architecturing components I) Initiator Core, II) Generations and III) Surface Functionality.

The name dendrimer is derived from Greek words *dendron* meaning "tree" and *meros* meaning "part".Dendrimersare large and complex molecules having verywell-definedchemical structures. They possess three distinguishing architecturalcomponents, mainly

(a) A Central Core Unit

(b) An interior layer(generations), composed of repeating units, radially attached to theinitiator core and

(c) Exterior (terminal functionality) attached tothe outermost interior generation as shown in Figure 8. [32].

**a) Central Core Unit:**

Central core unit is a multifunctional moiety present at the focal point of the structure and effects shape of the dendrimer. A core unit can be an atom or a big large molecule. It may be homogenous with other components of dendrimer or heterogeneous means may be Metal atom, Chromophore tec. It is the fundamental to blocks of dendrimer known as dendrons are attached. Its size, shape, multiplicity and specialized functional group will clearly influence dendritic architecture. The core unit may include chelating groups, molecular recognition moieties or hydrophobic / hydrophilic domains for desired properties. Therefore, Selection of Central Core has great importance.

### b) Interior Layers or Generations

The interior layers are produced by repetitive attachment of repeating or propagating units of building blocks to the core unit or previous layer. These layers are called generation of dendrimers. The repeating or propagating building block is an $AB_x$type monomer, which coupled with central core to yield exponential growth in both molecular weight and end group functionality of the dendrimer. The symmetric properties of the building blocks affects the overall properties of the dendrimer. If branched lengths are equal then the terminal groups are placed on the surface of an ideal circle and structure of dendrimer will be spherical.

### C) Terminal groups or surface functionality

In the point of view of applications, surface functional groups of dendrimers are of central importance for many applications of the dendrimers. The efficacy of dendrimer depends upon number and type of such functional group as they are exposed to outer layer. The number of such functional groups depends upon multiplicity of core unit and the repeating units of the dendrimer. These functional groups could be transformed into desirable functional groups as per the necessity for their particular applications by chemical methods.

## 1.4. Theoretical Aspects of Dendrimer

First ever report on theoretical aspects of dendrimer was published by De Gennes et al about the position of the end groups of the dendrimer [13]. De Gennes et al. used a self-consistent model in which the each generations are assumed to be fully elongated in which end groups of the dendrimers are circled around the central core. The mathematical prediction by de Gennes showed that there is a limit beyond which branching can no longer occur in ideal [13] way and the concept of starburst dense packing was attained [33, 34]. It also revealed that the core of the dendrimer has the lower density than the periphery. However, Lescanec and Muthukur predicts a monotonic decrease in the density on going from central core to surface [35]. This indicates that the ends of branches are not positioned at the surface but are back folded. Mansfield et al. [36] quantitatively showed the similar results by Monte Carlo simulation. Muret et al. [37] further showed an increase in back folding with generation number and a strong effect of solvent polarity on the radius of gyration of the dendrimers by molecular dynamics study. Boris et al. [38] predicted that the density is highest in the core and the end groups are distributed throughout the volume of dendritic polymers. Thus almost all the theoratical aspects showed the back folding of branches in dendrimer.

## 1.5. Effect of Core and Branching Multiplicity

The number of building blocks or branched cells, number of surface or terminal functional groups, molar mass and degree of polymerization of the dendrimer are directly related to the functionality/ multiplicity of Core(**C**) and branching units/ building blocks(**b**) as a functional of generation number(n). The values can be predicted mathematically for an ideal system according to following equation [32].

Number of Terminal Groups, $X = C \cdot b^n$

Number of Branch Cell, $y = C(b^n-1)/(b-1)$

Number of repeating unit of Degree of polymerization,

$Z = C(b^{n+1}-1)/(b-1)$

Theoretical molar Mass,

$M = M_c + C[\{M_{ru}(b^{n+1}-1)/(b-1)\} + M_t b^{n+1}]$ or

$M = M_c + C[\{M_{bc}(b^{n+1}-1)/(b-1)\} + M_t b^n]$

Where $M_c$, $M_{ru}$ or $M_{bc}$ and $M_t$ are the molar masses of the core, repeating units or branch cells and the terminal cells respectively. The size, shape, and central core functionality the final critical molecular design parameters of dendrimer.

## 1.6. Properties of Dendrimer Compared To Linear Polymers"

### 1.6.1. Dispersity

Traditional linear polymers are prepared by either conventional free radical polymerization or condensation polymerization. Such a conventional polymerization process is random in nature therefore it produces molecules of different size and molecular weight. So, traditional polymers are usually polydisperse. But Dendrimers are synthesized in a way such that their molecular weight and size are specifically controlled during synthesis. Themonodispersityofdendrimershas been extensively verified by high performance liquidchromatography (HPLC), size exclusion chromatography (SEC),mass spectrometry (MS), gel electrophoresis and transmissionelectron microscopy (TEM) [39]. Generally Convergently synthesized dendrimers are more likely to be mono disperse than divergently synthesized dendrimers [40]. The monodispersity of dendrimers are affected by two factors:

1. Dendrimer bridging during synthesis

2. Incomplete Removal of excess of reagent during generation sequences.

The latter factor can be easily seen during synthesis of PAMAM dendrimer, the incomplete removal of Ethylene diamine can lead to polydisperity of dendrimer as presence of unreacted ethylene diamine in 1st generation PAMAM dendrimer can function as an initiator core during further propagation [32].

### 1.6.2 Instristic Viscosity:

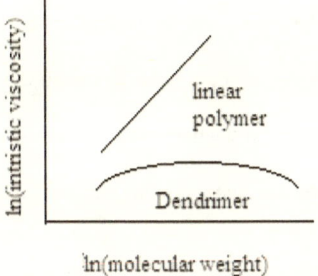

**Figure 9.** Co-relation between Instristic Viscosity and Molecular Weight.

In solution, linear polymeric chains exist as flexible coils; in contrast, dendrimers form a tightly packedball. This has a great impact on their rheologicalproperties. Dendrimer solutions have significantlylower viscosity than linear polymers [41].When the molecular mass of dendrimersincreases,their intrinsic viscosity goes through amaximum at the fourth generation and then begins to decline [42]. Such behavior is different compared thatof linear polymers. For classical polymers the intrinsicviscosity increases continuously with molecularmass. Such a relationship is shown in above figure 7.

### 3.3 Nanometer size:

Compared to traditional linear polymers, dendrimers have nanometer size and shape.Within the PAMAM dendrimer family, the diameter of the generation 1–10 with ethylenediamine core increases from 1.1 to 12.4nm[43].The shape persistence of dendrimers is veryimportant, as it allows the defined placement of functions not only on the dendrimer surface but also inside the dendritic voids. The PAMAM dendrimers of lower generation (G0–G3) withethylenediamine core have ellipsoidal shapes, whereas thePAMAMdendrimer of higher generation (G4–G10) have roughly spherical shapes [43]. X-ray analysis on dendrimeraggregateshave been revealed that the molecular shape of the lower tohigher generations becomes increasingly globular i.e. more sphericalcompare to linear shaped, in order to spread out the largermolecular structure with a minimal repulsion between the segments[44]. These fundamental properties have in fact lead to their commercial use for gene therapy, immunodiagnosticsand variety of other biological applications [45].

### 1.6.4. Polyvalency:

Polyvalency shows the outward presentation of reactive groups on the dendrimer nanostructure exterior. This creates more connections between surfaces and bulk materials for applications such as adhesives, surface coatings, or polymer cross-linking. The product, a topical vaginal microbicide called Vivagel™, prevents infection by HIVand other sexually transmitted diseases during intercourse takes advantage of dendrimers polyvalent properties.Depending upon which functional groups are present to the surface of a dendrimer's branches, thesenanostructures can behave like molecular Velcro. Simultaneously these functional groups can participate in multiple interactions with receptors on biological structures like cell membranes and virus [45].

Comparison of Properties of Dendrimer and linear polymers is given in table below.

Table 2. Properties of Dendrimer and linear polymers

| Sr. No. | Property | Dendrimers | Linear Polymers |
|---------|----------|------------|-----------------|
| 1 | Structure | Compact, Globular | Not compact |
| 2 | Synthesis | Careful & stepwise growth | Single step polycondensation |
| 3 | Structural control | Very high | Low |
| 4 | Architecture | Regular | Irregular |
| 5 | Shape | Spherical | Random coil |
| 6 | Crystallanity | Non-crystalline, amorphous materials  -lower glass temperatures | Semi crystalline/crystalline materials  -Higher glass temperatures |
| 7 | Aqueous solubility | High | Low |

| 8 | Nonpolar solubility | High | Low |
|---|---|---|---|
| 9 | Viscosity | Non linear relationship with molecular weight | Linear relation with molecular weight |
| 10 | Reactivity | High | Low |
| 11 | Compressibility | Low | High |
| 12 | Polydispersity | Monodisperse | Polydisperse |

## 1.7. Significance

Dendrimers are unique that they possess unique architectural features in their structures which are described earlier. The surface groups of dendrimers can also be changed from one functionality to other by appropriate and simple method. Thus the nature and the properties could be controlled easily as per requirement. Because of their unique structural features like no entanglement, high surface functionalities, etc. they possess a large variety of unusual properties like low viscosity, high reactivity, high solubility, interior cavity etc. The dendrimers are monodisperse, which is one of their most important property. The dense packing concept is one that once a specific generation number is reached, the space available for attachment of the next layer is less than that require by all the monomer that will fill that layer. Therefore the surface becomes "densely packed" and regular growth is stopped with incomplete functionalization of the terminal layer. Thus there is significant void space within the molecule.

This unique geometry has number of practical interesting and useful properties. For example, the densely packed dendrimer would be capable of entrapping guest molecule that could be slowly released through the crowded surface layer, useful for a novel drug delivery system [46-48], controlled release and pesticides [49], fertilizers [50] and mosquito repellents [51].

Dendrimers do not follow the well-known Mark Houwink equation, $[\eta]= kM^a$, especially at higher molecular weight. It was evident from number of different studies in their enhanced solubility when compared to functionality corresponding to linear polymers. One of the most important properties of dendrimer is exponential increase in number of end groups and molecular mass as a function of generation with increase in size.

Another significance of the dendrimers is that they bring active functional groups in close proximity. They are constrained by the architecture of the molecule to be at high concentration. The dendrimer have shown more functionality in closer vicinity to the surface where a chemical or a physical process takes place. Studies have shown that biocidal moieties work more efficiently when attached to dendritic molecule compared to free state in solution [52].

## References

1. Polymer Science, http://en.wikipedia.org/wiki/Polymer_science.

2. http://www.thehistoryblog.com/archives/6066.

3. "Bakelite: The World's First Synthetic Plastic". National Historic Chemical Landmarks. American Chemical Society. Retrieved June 25, 2012.

4. "Hermann Staudinger: Foundation of Polymer Science". National Historic Chemical Landmarks. American Chemical Society. Retrieved June 25, 2012.

5.  "U.S. Synthetic Rubber Program". National Historic Chemical Landmarks. American Chemical Society. Retrieved June 25, 2012.

6.  "Herman Mark and the Polymer Research Institute". National Historic Chemical Landmarks. American Chemical Society. Retrieved June 25, 2012.

7.  D. J. Cram, J. M. Cram; Science, **183**, 803, **(1974)**.

8.  F. Vogtle, E. Bhuleier, W. Wehner; Synthesis, 155, **(1978)**.

9.  R. G. Denkewalter, J. Kolc, W. J. Lukasavage; Preparation of lysine based macromolecular highly branched compound, U.S. Patent No. 4,360,646 **(1979)**.

10. R. G. Denkewalter, J. Kolc, W. J. Lukasavage; Macromolecular highly branched homogeneous compound based on lysine units, U.S. Patent No. 4,289,872 **(1981)**.

11. R. G. Denkewalter, J. Kolc, W. J. Lukasavage; Macromolecular highly branched homogeneous compound, U.S. Patent No. 4,410,688 **(1983)**.

12. M. Maciejewski, Macromol. Sci. Chem.1982, A17, 689–703.

13. P. G. De Gennes, H. J. Hervet; Journal de Physique –Lettres, **44**, 351, **(1983)**.

14. D. A. Tomalia; Adv. Mater., **6**, 529, **(1994)**.

15. D. A. Tomalia, A. Naylor, W. A. Goddard III, *Angew. Chem. 102*, 119**(1990)**.

16. P.-G. de Gennes, Angew. Chem. **104**, 856 **(1992)**; Angew. Chem. Int. Ed., **31**, 842**(1992)**.

17. D. A. Tomalia, H. Baker, J. R. Dewald, M. Hall, G. Kallos, S. Martin, J. Roeck, J. Ryder, P. Smith, *Polym. J., 17*,117**(1985)**.

18. G. R. Newkome, Z.-Q. Yao, G. R. Baker, V.K. Gupta, J. Org. Chem. **50**, 2003 **(1985)**.

19. G.R. Newkome, C. N. Moorefield, F. Vögtle, Dendrimers and Dendrons, Wiley-VCH, Weinheim, 1st Edit.**(2001).**

20. C. Hawker, J. M. J. Fréchet, J. Chem. Soc., Chem. Commun. 1010, **(1990)**.

21. T. M. Miller, T. X. Neenan, Chem. Mater. **2**, 346 **(1990)**.

22. J.M.J. Frechet, D.A. Tomalia. Dendrimers and other Dendritic polymers. John Wiley and sons.**(2001)**.

23. F. Vogtle, G. Richardt, N. Werner. Dendrimer Chemistry: Concepts, Synthesis, Properties, Applications. Wiley WCH. **2009**.

24. D.A. Tomalia. Macromole Symp. 101, 243, **(1996)**.

25. D.A. Tomalia, H.M. Brothers II, L.T. Piehler, Y. Hsu. Polymer Mater Sci. Eng. **73**, 75**(1995)**.

26. P.R. Dvornic, D.A. Tomalia. Science Spectra. **5**, 36, **(1996)**.

27. A.K. Naj. Persistent Inventor Markets a Molecule, New York, B1, **(1996)**.

28. T. Emrick, J. M. J. Frechet. Curr. Opin. Colloid. Interface. Sci. 4, 15**(1999)**.

29. D. A. Tomalia, D.M. Hedstrand, M.S. Ferritto. Macromolecules. 24, 1435**(1991)**.

30. C. J. Hawker, J.M.J Frechet. J. Am Chem. Soc., **112**, 7638**(1990)**.

31. C. J. Hawker, K.L. Wooley, J.M.J Frechet. J. Chem. Soc. Perkins Trans. **1**, 1287**(1993)**.

32. D.A. Tomalia, H. Baker, J. Dewald, M. Hall, G. Kallos, S. Martin, J. Roeck, J. Ryder, P. Smith, Polym. J. **17**, 117 **(1985)**.

33. J.S. Moore, Z. Xu. Macromolecules, **24**, 5893, **(1991)**.

34. Y. Wang, F. Zeng, S.C. Zimmerman. Tetrahedron Lett, **38**, 5459 **(1997)**.

35. R.L. Lescanec, M. Muthukumar. Macromolecules. **23**, 2280, **(1990)**.

36. M. L. Mansfield, L.I. Klushin. Macromolecules, **26**, 4262, **(1993)**.

37. M. Murat, G.S. Grest. Macromolecules. **29**, 1278, **(1996)**.

38. D. Boris, M. Rubinstien, Macromolecules. **29**, 1996, **(7251)**.

39. J.L. Jackson, H.D. Chanzy, F.P. Booy, B.J. Drake, D.A. Tomalia, B.J. Bauer, E.J. Amis. Macromolecules.,**31**,6259**(1998)**.

40. D. A. Tomalia. Prog. Polym. Sci. **30**, 294 **(2005)**.

41. J.M.J.Fréchet, Science. **263**, 1710**(1994)**.

42. T.H.Mourey, S.R. Turner, M. Rubenstein,J.M.J. Fréchet, C.J. Hawker, K.L. Wooley.Macromolecules. **25**, 2401**(1992)**.

43. Y. Cheng, N. Man, T. Xu, R. Fu, X. Wang, X. Wang, L. Wen. J. Pharm. Sci. **96**, 595**(2007)**.

44. V.Percec, W.D. Cho, P.E.Mosier, G. Ungar, D.J.P. Yeardley. J. Am. Chem. Soc. 120,11061 **(1998)**.

45. C.Bieniarz,"Dendrimers: applications to pharmaceutical and medicinal chemistry. In: Encyclopedia of Pharmaceutical Technology." Marcel Dekker, New York, 1998. 55–89.

46. R. Langer, Chem. Eng. Sci. **50**, 4109**(1995)**.

47. R. Duncan, J. Kopecek, Adv. Polym. Sci. **57**, 51**(1984)**.

48. P. A. Brandy, E. G. Levy. Chem. Ind. (London) **18**, 21, **(1995)**.

49. M.M. Schreiber, B.S. Sharha, D. Trimmel, M.D. White. 'Method of applying Herbicides, Controlled Release Herbicides', WSS, A monograph, Weed Society of America, P.177 **(1987)**

50. N. Karak, J. Polym. Mater. **16**, 309**(1999)**.

51. A.J. Domb, A. Marlinsky, M. Maniar, I. Teomin, J. Am. Mosquito Control. Assoc. **11**, 29**(1995)**.

52. C.Z. Chen, N.C. BeckTan, S.L. Cooper. Chem. Commun., 1585**(1999)**.

# 2. DENDRIMER SYNTHESIS

## 2.1. Introduction

A Dendrimer can be constructed by a vast range of routes. In general dendrimer synthesis involve ordered assembly strategies that requires following architecturing components.

Many methods for assembling these architecturing components have been reported. These methods however can be classified into two categories: Divergent method and Convergent method.

Historically early reported synthesis of dendrimers were based on divergent methods. In divergent method dendrimer was constructed from core to surface. Fritz Vogtle et al. first reported synthesis of Polypropyleneimine [PPI] type of dendrimer though limited up to generation two using divergent method [1]. However, synthesis up to higher generations were not possible as reported by Vogtle due to analytical and synthetic difficulties [2]. Almost simultaneously Tomalia et al. reported first completely characterized series of Polyamidoamine type dendrimers which were synthesized up to generation 10 by divergent method [3,4]. First example of convergent route can be traced in early 1990s which was developed by Hawker and Frechet [5]. In this technique, dendrimer is grown inward i.e. from surface to core i.e. several dendrons are constructed in first step and then reacted with multifunctionalized core to give dendrimer. Both of these routes may require either functional group interconversion or protection / deprotections. Over 100 compositionally differentdendrimer familieshavebeensynthesizedandover1000differentiated                chemical surfacemodificationshavebeenreported, mainly on the basis of these two syntheticroutes[6-9].

## 2.2. Traditional Routes

### 2.2.1.Divergent Growth

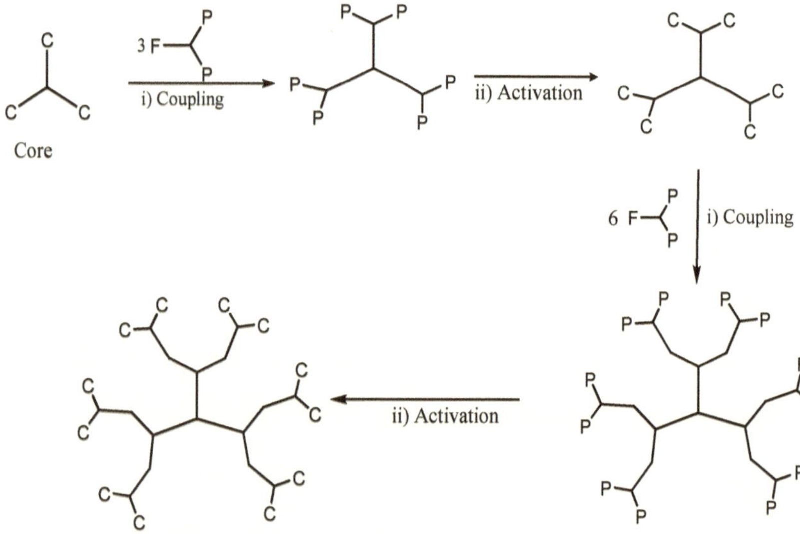

**Fig. 1** Shows "Divergent Approach" (Where F= Unprotected functional group, P= Protected functional group and C= Coupling point)

In divergent approach, synthesis of dendrimer starts from a multi-functionalized initiator core (Fig. 1), to which multi-functionalized branching units or monomers are attached in first step. During this reaction surface functionality of this branching units are deactivated or protected. After completion of first step these surface groups are activated or unprotected, which undergoes further reaction. These iterative reactions steps are repeated until desired generation of dendrimer is obtained and a dendrimer grows outwards from core to surface. Moreover, as the dendrimer grows larger, the end groups on the surface become more and more closely packed and because of steric hindrance, the dendrimer reaches its upper generation limit. This is known as the "de Gennes dense packing"[10] named after Pierre-Gilles de Gennes or "starburst effect" named by Tomalia [11].

Advantage of using this route is attainable high molecular weight with possibility of automation in repetition steps. A significant disadvantage of this method is that no of terminal groups in growing dendrimer increases exponentially, so it cannot be made to always made to react quantitatively which leads to structural defects. Also purification and separation of dendrimer from excess of reagents is problematic due to similar properties [12].

Polyamidoamine(PAMAM) and Polypropylene imine (PPI) classes of dendrimers were prepared by using this route.

### 2.2.3.Convergent Route

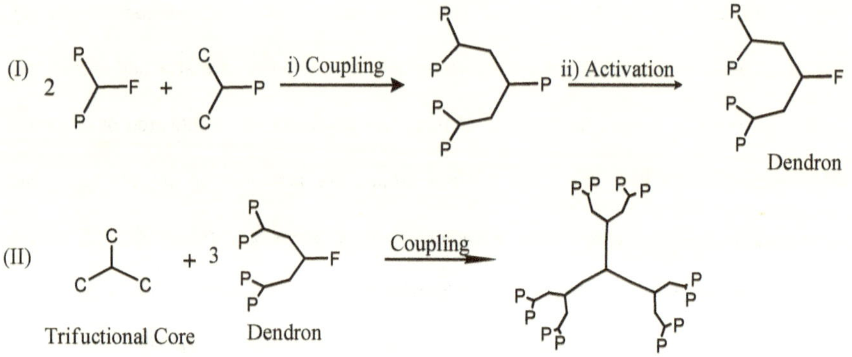

**Fig. 2**Shows "Convergent Approach" (Where C= Coupling point, P= Protected focal point and F= Unprotected or activated focal point)

Hawker and Fréchet [5] developed the convergent methodology, which assembles the macromolecule from the outside to finish at the core. Convergent growth generally starts from surface unit which coupled with a monomer unit to give a dendron whose focal point is deactivated or protected (Fig. 2). In the second step of reaction the focal point becomes activated for further reaction, and the dendron is grown inwards. At the end of the reaction these highly branched dendrons reacted to a multi functionalized core to give a dendrimer.

Unlike divergent growth this method does not produce structural defects which was observed earlier with divergent method. Moreover this method can be performed in equi-molar quantities so purification as separation steps are relatively easy. The dimensions of dendrimer growth are subject to limitations set by steric-hindrance during reaction of the dendrons at the periphery. So this method is used mainly for low molecular weight dendrimers [12].

## 2.3.Recent Methods

### 2.3.1.Double exponential growth

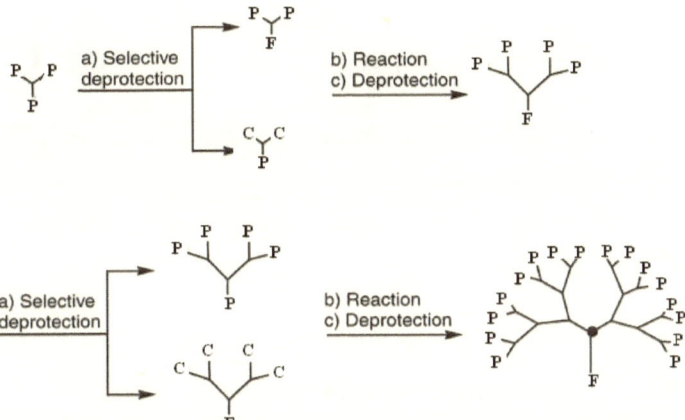

**Fig. 3**shows "Double Exponential Growth" (Where C=Coupling group, F=Functional group,and

P=Protected group)

The double-exponential method can basically be regarded as a convergent growth strategy for

a Dendron [13, 14]. This approach involves growth of dendron in two directions:

1. Growth inwards towards core by focal point activation and

2. Growth towards surface by surface group activation.

A branching moiety containing two coupling sites both are completely protected undergoes

selective deprotection. In two completely separate steps, branching unit in one step undergoes

surface deprotection where as in other step it undergoes focal point deprotection. Now both

unprotected dendrons arereacted in second step to give second generation dendron. Iteration

of the synthetic sequence leads to the corresponding fourth-generation dendron.

**2.3.2 Hypercore or Hypermonomer Approach**

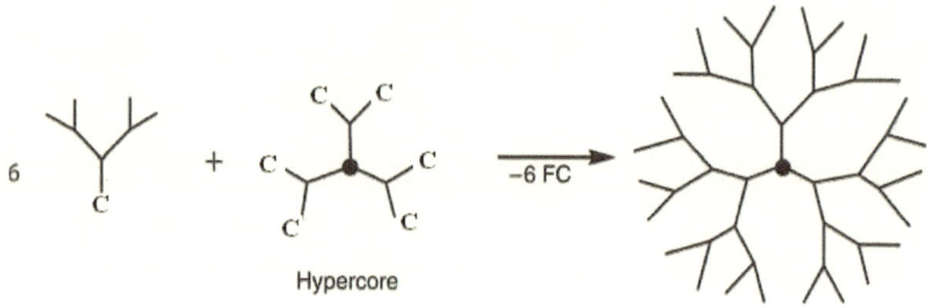

**Fig. 4**. Shows "Hypercores" or "Branched Monomers" Growth (Where C= Functional Group, F= Activated focal Point and P= Protected focal point)

Frechet et al. [15] focused on acceleration of dendrimer synthesis. The outcome of this research was "Hypercores" approach. These methods involve the pre assembly of olingomeric species, which can then be linked together to give dendrimers in fewer steps or higher yields, taking advantage of the best points of both the convergent and the divergent technique. The "Hypercore" and "Branched Monomer" are pre-branched analogues of the cores and dendrons that are used in "Traditional" dendrimer syntheses.

Fig. 4 shows how they could be utilized in the synthesis of large dendritic structures. The wedge is constructed by reaction of a surface unit with a branched monomer in one step followed by focal point activation in second step. Hypercore is constructed by divergent growth of core in single step. These surface activated hypercore and focal point activated wedge can be reacted in a single step to give fourth generation dendrimer.

**2.3.3. Orthogonal Coupling Strategy**

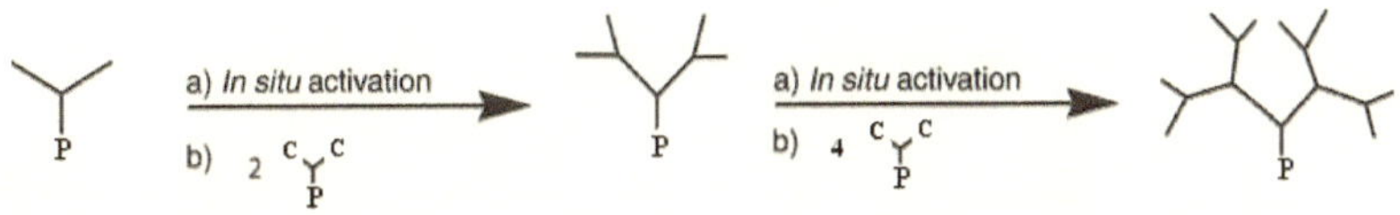

**Fig. 5** Shows "Orthogonal Coupling Strategy" (Where P= Protecting group which on *in situ*

activation is converted into C= Functional group which spontaneously undergoes Reaction)

In an orthogonal synthesis two different branching units with complementary coupling

functions are used alternating and no activation step is employed [16-17]. The selected

reactants as well as the resulting coupling product must be inert towards the subsequent

reaction conditions. The term orthogonal means that the functionalities are initially inert

towards the coupling conditions, but can be activated *in situ* for the desired subsequent

reaction or coupling.

As shown in Fig. 6, If this conditions are met, a dendrimer can be constructed either by

divergent or convergent method in just a few steps.

However, the method of orthogonal coupling has still not been very widely adopted because

the building blocks used have to meet very stringent structural requirements [19]. Spindler and

Fréchet [17] were the first to prepare a third-generation polyethercarbamate dendron in a one-

pot synthesis. Zeng and Zimmerman [20] reported the first application of orthogonal coupling

to the synthesis of higher generation dendrimer. Freeman and Frechet [21] reported

convergent synthesis of poly (benzyl ester) dendrimer and Shimanek et al. [22] reported

synthesis of melamine based dendrimer by using orthogonal coupling strategy.

An advantage of such method is that it does not involve protecting group manipulations and functional group interconversion.

### 2.3.4.Lego Chemistry

In "Lego chemistry" strategy, highly functionalized cores and branched monomers are applied to prepare phosphorus dendrimers. The end groups are generally phosphines and hydrazines. Generation 4 is synthesized in only 4 Steps and no. surface group increases from 48 to 250. This synthesis requires minimum volume of solvent, allow facile purification and produce environmentally benign by products such as water and nitrogen [23].

### 2.3.5Click chemistry

In 2001, Sharpless et al. [24] proposed this method in which smaller units are joined together by way of heteroatom bonds as a fast track route to compounds. Typical reactions applied are 1,3-dipolar cycloadditions, nucleophilic substitutions for ring opening of strained electrophilic heterocycles, as well as additions to carbon-carbon multiple bonds e.g. epoxidation. Azide functionalized PAMAM dendrons were produced by convergent method using click chemistry [25].Wooley and Hawker et al. [26] synthesized second and third-generation dendrimers with a "divergent click strategy". A first-generation azido- dendrimer was converted in a Cu(I)-catalysed reaction with an alkynylated monomer into a triazole dendrimer with terminal hydroxyl groups, which in turn were converted in a second step into azido functions, in order to again undergo repetitive reaction with alkynylated monomers [27]. Unprotected glycol-dendrimers, peptido- and redox-dendrimers and dendronized polymer organogels can also be prepared by click chemistry [28].

### 2.3.6. Solid Phase Synthesis

Solid phase synthetic methodology was first established by Merrifield in 1963 in the area of peptide synthesis [29].

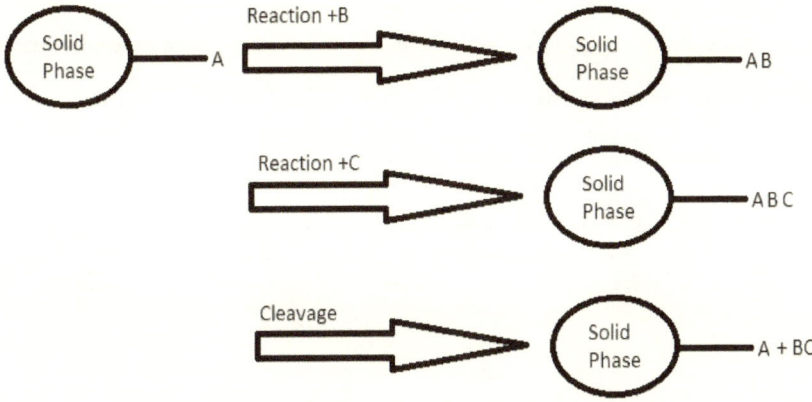

**Figure 6.** Solid-phase synthesis (schematic); for the sake of simplicity only one of the many functional groups (A) attached to a solid phase bead is shown

The synthetic scheme shown in Fig. 6 proceeds in the first step as a covalentcoupling of substrate (*B*) *via* a linker to the functional group *A* (*e.g.* –NH2)attached in a prior step to a commercially available solid phase. This solid phaseusually consists of an insoluble polymeric material, with polystyrene most frequentlyserving as the polymeric support – generally in the form of beads. Critical condition for optimum reaction are good swelling properties of the support material: the greater the swelling, the greater the surface area availablefor chemical reactions.eaction of the new substrate C with the previously coupled substrate (*solid phase–A–B*) is followed either by (generally hydrolytic)cleavage of the product *B–C* formed on the solid phase from the support, or byfurther reaction with substrates *D, E, F*, to give a linear sequence

*B–C–D–E–F* –or isomers thereof with the letters in a different order – should the substrate solutions be added in a different order.

An advantage of solid phase synthesis is excess amount of reactant can be used and the yields can increased. Reaction work up and purification is relatively easier compared to homogeneous reaction which requires simple filtration. Polymeric support materials can also be recycled which is beneficial.

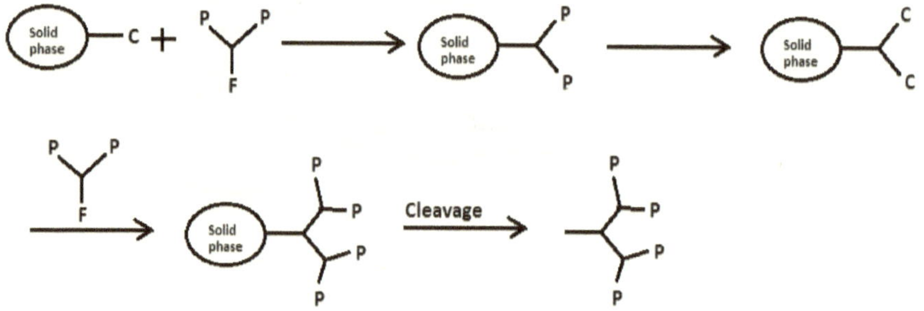

**Figure 7.** Synthesis of dendrimer on solid phase.

In dendrimer synthesis, solid-phase synthesis has been used primarily for the synthesis of peptideand glycopeptide dendrimers [30]. A second generation dendrimer could be prepared by successive addition of branchedpolyproline building blocks to a solid phase [31]. Frechet et al. accomplished synthesis of Polyamidoamine dendrimers on polystyrene [32] in 1991 [33]. PAMAM dendrons could be developed up to the fourth generation [34]. Solid-phase synthesis was also employed for polylysine dendrimers, whose basic structures are used as "multiple antigen peptides" (MAP) [35]. Resin-bonded polylysine dendrimers have meanwhile become commerciallyavailable.

**2.3.7.Supramolecular Synthesis**

In contrast to the methods already explained, the supramolecular synthesis [36] of dendrimers does not involve covalent bond formation, but instead it involves non-covalent interactions. Fréchet et al. were able to coordinate polyether dendrons having carboxylate functional groups at the focal point with lanthanide ions up to the fourth generation [figure 8] [37]. Synthesis by straightforward ligand exchange starting from lanthanide triacetates with dendron carboxylates was made possible by thepredominantly ionic – and reversible – interactions between the lanthanide ion bearing a triple positive charge and carboxylate groups.

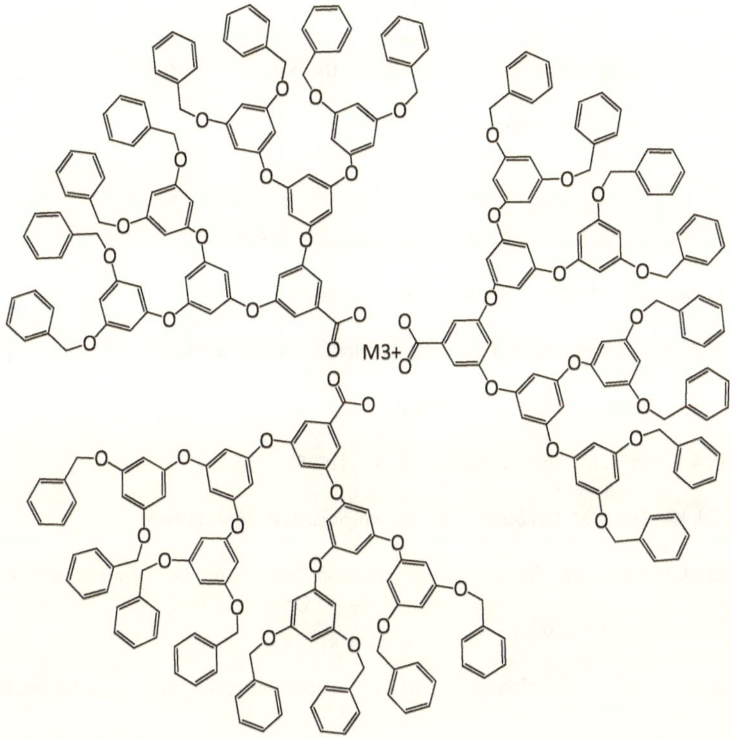

**Figure 8.** Lanthanide ion as core unit of a dendritic metal complex where $M^{3+}$= Er, Eu, Tb.

Smith et al. reported "A two component dendritic gelator" on the basis of self-assembling acid-base/hydrogen bond interactions. Dendritic lysinebuilding blocks serve as dendrons, and an aliphatic diamine as core (Fig. 9).Depending upon the choice of building blocks, the supramolecular complexforms fibrous gel phases by self-organisation. The dendritic peptides used with d- and l-lysine building blocks each containthree stereocentres. The chirality of d- and l-lysine exerts a controlling effect onstructure during self-assembly in the gel fibres and hence on the morphologyand macroscopic properties of the product. LLL- or DDD enantiomeric units leadto fibres, whereas the corresponding racemic gels are more prone to form planarstructures. The chirality accordingly affects the pattern of hydrogen bondingduring the formation of molecular aggregates [38].

## References

1.  F. Vogtle, E. Bhuleier, W. Wehner; Synthesis, 155, **(1978)**.

2.  R. Moores, F. Vogtle. Chem. Ber. **126,** 2133, **(1993)**

3.  D. A. Tomalia, H. Baker, J. Dewald, M. Hall, G. Kallos, S. Martin, J. Roeck, J. Ryder, P. Smith; Polymer J., 1985, **17**, 117**(1986)**.

4.  D. A. Tomalia; Macromole. Sym., **101**, 243, **(1996)**.

5.  C. J. Hawker, J. M. J. Fréchet; J. Am. Chem. Soc., **112**, 7638, **(1990)**.

6.  J.M.J. Fréchet, D.A. Tomalia; Dendrimers and Other Dendritic Polymers. John Wiley & Sons, Chichester, **(2001)**.

7.  D.A. Tomalia, I. Majoros; Dendrimeric supra-molecular and suprmacromolecular assemblies. In: A.Ciferri, (Ed.); Supramolecular Polymers., Marcel Dekker, New York, 359 **(2000)**.

8. A.W. Bosman, H.M. Janssen, E.W. Meijer; Chem.Rev., 99, 1665 **(1999)**.

9. B.K. Nanjwade, H.M. Bechra, G.K. Derkar, F.V. Manvi, V.K. Nanjwade; Eur. J. Pharm. Sci., 38(3), 85 **(2009)**.

10. P. G. De Gennes, H. J. Hervet; Journal de Physique –Lettres, **44**, 351, **(1983)**.

11. D. A. Tomalia; Adv. Mater., **6**, 529, **(1994)**.

12. F. Vogtle, G. Richardt, N. werner, Dendrimer Chemistry: Concepts, Synthesis and Applications. **(2009)**, Wiley-VCH, Verlag.

13. C. J. Hawker, J. M. J. Frechet, *J. Chem. Soc., Chem. Commun.* **1990**, 1010–1013.

14. R. Klopsch, P. Franke, A. D. Schlüter; *Chem.-A Eur. J.*, **2**, 1330, **(1996)**.

15. T. Kawaguchi, K. L. Walker, C. L. Wilkins, J. S. Moore; J. Am. Chem. Soc., **117**, 2159, **(1995)**.

16. K. L. Wooley, C. J. Hawker, J. M. J. Fréchet; J. Am. Chem. Soc., **113**, 4252, **(1991)**.

17. R. Spindler, J. M. J. Frechet; J. Chem. Soc. Perkins Trans., **1**, 913, **(1993)**.

18. G. R. Newkome, C. N. Moorefield, F. Vögtle; Dendrimers and Dendrons: Concepts, Syntheses, Applications, Wiley-VCH, Weinheim, **(2001)**.

19. S. Greyson, J. M. J. Fréchet; Chemical Rev., **101**, 3819, **(2001)**.

20. F. Zeng, S. C. Zimmerman, J. Am. Chem. Soc., **118**, 5326, **(1996)**.

21. A.W. Freeman, J. M. J. Frechet, Org. Letters, **1**, 685, **(1999)**.

22. W. Zeng, D. T. Nowlan, L. M. Thomson, W. M. Lackowski, E. E. Shimanek, J. Am. Chem. Soc., **123**(37), 8914, **(2001)**.

23. V. Maraval, J. Pyzowski, A. M. Caminade, J. P. Mojoral; J. Org. Chem., **68**, 6043, **(2003)**.

24. H. C. Kolb, M. G. Finn, K. B. Sharpless; *Angew. Chem. Int. Ed.*, **40**(11), 2004, **(2001)**.

25. J. W. Lee, J. W. Kim, B. K. Kim, J. H. Kim, W. S. Shin, S. H. Jin; Tetrahedron, **62**(39), 9193, **(2006)**.

26. P. Wu, A. K. Feldman, A. K. Nugent, C. J. Hawker, A. Scheel, B. Voit, J. Pyun, J. M. J. Fréchet, K. B. Sharpless, V. V. Fokin, M. J. Joralemon, R. K. O'Reilly, J. B. Matson, A. K. Nugent, C. J. Hawker, K. L. Wooley, Macromolecules. **38**, 5436 **(2005)**.

27. M. Malkoch, K. Schleicher, E. Drockenmuller, C. J. Hawker, T. P. Russell, P. Wu, V. V. Fokin, Macromolecules. **38**, 3663**(2005)**.

28. E. Fernandez- Megia, J. Correa, I. Rodriguez-Meizoso, R. Riguera, Macromolecules. **39**, 2113 **(2006)**.

29. R. B. Merrifield, J. Am. Chem. Soc.,**85**, 2149**(1963)**.

30. P. Vepřek, J. Ježek, J. Peptide Sci.,**5**, 5**(1999)**.

31. G. Sanclimens, L. Crespo, E. Giralt, M.Royo, F. Albericio, Peptide Sci. **76**,283**(2004)**.

32. H.-F. T. K.-K. Mong, M. F. Nongrum, C.-W. Wan, Tetrahedron. **54**, 8543**(1998)**.

33. K. E. Uhrich, S. Boegemann, J. M. J.Fréchet, S. R. Turner, Polym. Bull. **25**, 551**(1991)**.

34. V. Swali, N. J. Wels, G. J. Langley, M.Bradley, J. Org. Chem.**62**, 4902**(1997)**.

35. D. N. Posnett, H. McGrath, J. P. Tam,J. Biol. Chem. **263**, 1719 **(1988)**.

36. K. Ariga,T. Kunitake, Supramolecular Chemistry –Fundamentals and Applications, Springer-Verlag, Berlin, Heidelberg,**(2006)**.

37. M. Kawa, J. M. J. Fréchet, Chem. Mater. **10**, 286**(1998)**.

38. A. R. Hirst, D. K. Smith, M. C. Feiters,H. P. M. Geurts, Chem. Eur. J. 10, 5901 **(2004)**.

# 3. APPLICATIONS

## 3.1. Introduction

Chapter-1 and Chapter-2 have discussed basic concepts of about dendrimer and synthetic routes for dendrimer synthesis. This chapter will explain different types of dendritic molecules as well their synthesis.

## 3.2. Types of Dendrimers

### 3.2.1. PPI Dendrimer

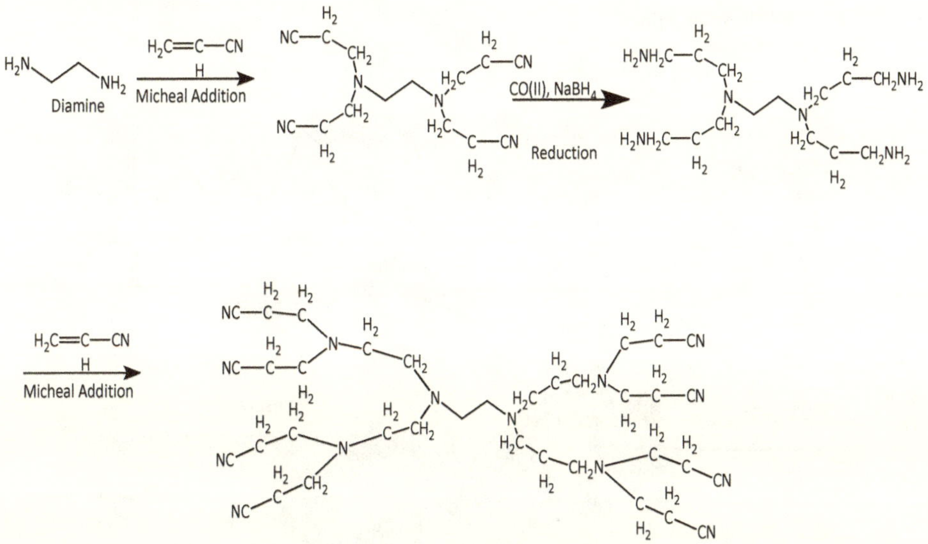

**Scheme. 1** Synthesis of PPI Dendrimers

The term "POPAM" or "PPI" is attributed to Polypropylene-imine class of dendrimers. Such class of dendrimers along with PAMAM dendrimer is most widely used and commercialized [01]. Synthesis of POPAM dendrimer is based on divergent route which was first developed by Voglte in 1978[2].Acrylonitrile is added to ethylene diamine which undergoes Micheal addition to give

half generation imine terminated dendrimer which in the second step undergoes reduction to

give amine terminated G1dendrimer [02]. These two iterative reaction steps are repeated until

desired generation of dendrimer is achieved. Although samples of such dendrimers are

assigned a high degree of purity by electrospray ionisation-mass spectrometry (ESI-MS) [03],

owing to divergent synthesisstructural defects can occur here through incomplete reaction

during Michael addition in 2nd step.The high degree of branching inhibits generation growth

from the fifth generation onwards as a result ofsteric hindrance.

### 3.2.2. PAMAM Dendrimer

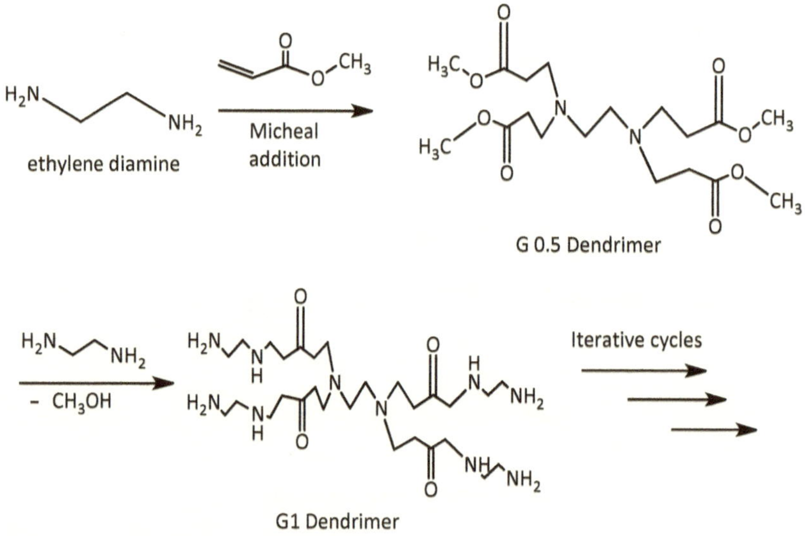

G 0.5 Dendrimer

G1 Dendrimer

**Scheme 2.** Synthesis of PAMAM dendrimer

The term "PAMAM" is abbreviated for Polyamido amine dendrimer. They are distinguished

from POPAM by amide bond present in molecule. They are also termed as "STARBURST" dendrimers. Such class of dendrimers was first synthesized by Tomalia et al in 1985. Synthesis

was initiated by using an ammonia core which undergoes micheal addition with methyl acrylate

to give ester terminated half generation dendrimer which in second step undergoes exhaustive

amidation with excess of ethylene diamine to give full generation dendrimer[4].They are often

less easy to prepare in such high purity, since back folding and defects in the dendrimer scaffold

occur despite the extended branches resulting from the presence of ethylenediamine as flexible

spacer clearly owing to hindered rotation around theamide bonds.The PAMAM limiting

generationis only reached at almost twice the generation number as in the case

ofPOPAMdendrimersi.e from the tenth generation onwards, however, the PAPAMsurface has

become so "dense" that further reactions run into problems.

### 3.2.3.POMAM Dendrimers

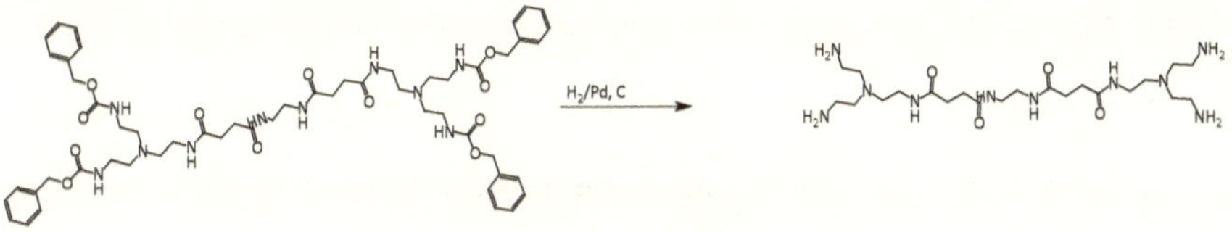

**Scheme 3.** Synthesis of POMAM Dendrimers

Dendritic hybrid architectures of the two dendrimer types POPAM and PAMAM designated by

Majoros et al. as "POMAM dendrimers" [5] are structural rarities. One such dendrimer of this

type was assembled with PAMAM branching units starting from a POPAM core unit [5].Starting

from a zeroth generation POPAM dendrimer, the protective group is removed by palladium-

catalysed hydrogenation to activate the amino groups. Subsequent reaction with a succinimide

ester as bearer of the AB2 coupling unit leads to a first-generation "hybrid dendrimer".

Repetition of this synthetic sequence provides an entry to higher-generation POMAM dendrimers as per Scheme 3.

### 3.2.4. PAMAM-OS Dendrimer

Radially layered poly (amidoamine-organosilicon) dendrimers (PAMAMOS) are inverted unimolecular micelles that consist of hydrophilic, nucleophilic polyamidoamine (PAMAM) interiors and hydrophobic organosilicon exteriors. These dendrimers are exceptionally useful precursors for the preparation of honeycomb like networks with nanoscopic PAMAM and Organosillicon domains [6].

### 3.2.5. Liquid Crystalline Dendrimers

They consist of liq. crystallinemonomerse.g. mesogenfunctionalizedcarbosilanedendrimers. Functionalization ofend group of carbosilanedendrimers with 36 mesogen i.e. units,attached through a C-5 spacer, leads to liquid crystalline dendrimersthat form broad smeticA phase in the temperature range of 17–130 ∘C [7]. Boiko et al. claims that theyhave synthesized first photosensitive liquid crystalline dendrimerwith terminal cinnamoyl groups. They have confirmed the structureand purity of this LC dendrimer by 1H NMR and GPC methods.It was shown that such a dendrimer, under UV irradiation, canundergo E-Z isomerization of the cinnamoyl groups and [2 + 2] photocycloadditionleading to the formation of a three-dimensional network [8].

### 3.2.6. Tecto Dendrimer

Tecto-dendrimers are composed of a core dendrimer, whichmay or may not contain the therapeutic agent, surrounded bydendrimers. The surrounding dendrimers are of several types, each type designed to perform a function necessary to a smart therapeutic nano-device [9].

### 3.2.7. Chiral dendrimer

The chirality in these dendrimers is based upon the construction of constitutionally different but chemically similar branches to chiral core. Such subclass of Dendrimers is important with potential application in asymmetric catalysis and chiral molecular recognition [10].

### 3.2.8. Hybrid Dendrimers

Hybrid polymers are combination of linear polymer and dendrimers in graft or co-polymer forms. The small dendritic segment combined with multiple reactive chain ends providesan opportunity to use them as surface active agents, compatibilizer adhesives, e.g. hybrid dendritic linear polymers [11].

### 3.2.9. Peptide Dendrimers

Dendrimers having peptides on the surface of the traditional dendrimer architecture and dendrimers incorporating amino acids as branching or core units are both defined as 'peptide dendrimers' [12].A dendrimer containing peptide bond in structure can also be called as 'peptide dendrimer'. Peptide dendrimers play an important role in diverse areas including cancer, antimicrobials, antiviral, central nervous system, analgesia, asthma, allergy and Ca+2metabolism. On the basis of their ability to be taken up by cells, making peptides very useful for drug delivery.

### 3.2.10. Polylysine Dendrimers

Polylysine dendrimers are largely characterized by amide bonds. They attracted interest as potential therapeutic agents for use in boron neutron capture therapy and in magnetic resonance imaging (MRI). Since dendritic polylysines apparently have a lower toxicity than their linear counterparts.Qualmann et al. [13] polylysines with a total of 80 terminal boron atoms in the carborane units and a dansyl group was designedspecifically for boron neutron capture therapy.

Synthesis of these dendrimers is performed by condensation of the aminoacid lysine, whose amino functions have previously been protected with tert-butyloxycarbonylgroups (Boc), onto an (activated) l-lysine p-nitrophenyl ester. Theresulting coupling product (Fig. 4.11) is then deprotected with trifluoroaceticacid and thus activated for renewed reaction. Iteration of the assembly andactivation step ultimately led to a polylysine dendrimer with 1024 terminal butyloxycarbonyl groups [14, 15, 16].

### 3.2.11. Glyco-dendrimers

The molecular scaffolds of carbohydrate dendrimers can be varied in many different ways: carbohydrates can act as core unit, serve for branching, or function as terminal groups [17].The first glycodendrimer was pepared by Roy et al. [18, 19]. Access to dendrimers bearing carbohydrate terminal groups is provided by the triglycosylated trihydroxyamine [20] obtained in a several-stage synthesis, which can serve as dendron.The amino dendrons could be attached to the tricarboxylic acid core byDCC coupling (dicyclohexylcarbodiimide)[21].

Glycopeptide dendrimers with carbohydrate units both in the core and in the branching units were prepared by Lindhorst et al. via a generalisable synthetic route [22]. The first PAMAM dendrimer with a carbohydrate core unit was prepared from the -d-glycoside as coreunit precursor. Up to second-generation PAMAM dendrimers with a d-glucosecore could be prepared by iteration [23].

### 3.3. Applications of Dendrimer

### 3.3.1. Dendrimer as Carrier for Drug Delivery

Dendrimers led several groups to investigate the possibilityof encapsulating drugmoleculeswithin thebranches of a dendrimer. This offers the potential ofdendrimers tointeractwithlabileorpoorlysoluble drugs, enhancedrugstability,bioavailabilityand controllingitsrelease.Nature of drug binding maybe either physical encapsulation into internal cavitiesof dendrimerormaybe co-valent bond formation to the periphery of dendrimer [24, 25, 26].

### 3.3.1.1. Dendrimers in Ocular Drug Delivery

Anatomy and physiology of eye make it a very delicate and highly important organ. Designing an effective therapy for ocular diseases particularly for posterior region has considered a formidable task [27]. Eye contains various types of barriers such as different layers of cornea, sclera and retina including blood aqueous and blood–retinal barriers, choroidal and conjunctival blood flow etc. These barriers cause a significant challenge for delivery of a drug alone or in a dosage form, especially to the posterior segment of the eye [28]. The nano-size, ease of preparation, functionalization, and possibility to attach multiple surface groups renders dendrimers as suitable alternative vehicle of ophthalmic drug delivery [29-31]. Recent research efforts for improving residence time of pilocarpine in the eye was increased by using poly (amidoamine) dendrimers with carboxylic or hydroxyl surface groups [32]. These surface-modified dendrimers were predicted to enhance pilocarpine & tropicamide bioavailability [33]. Also some of the phosphorus containing dendrimers with quaternary ammonium core and terminal carboxylic groups has successfully reported for ocular drug delivery of carteolol [34]. Yao et al. [35]have prepared and characterized the complex of puerarin and poly (amidoamine) (PAMAM) dendrimers and to evaluate the complex as an ocular drug delivery system. The results showed that puerarin-dendrimer complexes formed primarily by hydrogen-bonding interactions. Typically, 43, 56, 125, and 170 molecules of puerarin could be incorporated into G3.5, G4, G4.5, and G5 PAMAM dendrimer molecule. Puerarin was released more slowly from puerarin-dendrimer complexes than free puerarin in deionized water and phosphate buffer solution (pH 6.8). Furthermore, 310 puerarin-dendrimer complexes produced longer ocular residence times compared with puerarin eye drops. No damages to the epithelium or endothelium were observed after the PAMAM dendrimer administration in this corneal permeation study. These results indicate that dendrimers are potential carriers for ophthalmic drug delivery.

### 3.3.1.2. Dendrimer in Transdermal Drug Delivery

Transdermal drug delivery has made an important contribution to medical practice, but yet to fully achieve it's potential as an alternative to oral delivery and hypodermic injections [36]. A way to improve transdermal drug delivery is to use transdermal enhancers which increase permeation through skin. Therefore, polymeric enhancers with hydrophilic and hydrophobic groups like PAMAM dendrimers have attracted increasing interest. Wang et al. [37] reported the utilization of polyhydroxyalkanoate (PHA) and G3 PAMAM dendrimer as novel transdermal drug delivery systems. Tamsulosin hydrochloride was utilised as model drug and it was concluded that PHA-dendrimer matrix can be utilised as drug delivery systems. Yiyun et al. [38] reported that Poly (amidoamine) dendrimer complex with Non-steroidal Anti-inflammatory Drugs (NSAIDs) e.g. Ketoprofen, Diflunisal could be improving the drug permeation through the skin as penetration enhancers. Ketoprofen and Diflunisal were conjugated with G5 Poly (amidoamine) dendrimer and showed 3.4 and 3.2 times higher permeation. Chauhan et al. [39]

investigated enhanced bioavailability of Poly (amidoamine) (PAMAM) dendrimer by using indomethacin as the model drug in transdermal drug delivery. Borowska et al. [40] have assessed the ability of (PAMAM) dendrimers G3 and G4 to facilitate transdermal delivery of 8-methoxypsoralen (8-MOP) in vivo. In vitro study using Franz diffusion cell revealed an enhanced transdermal flux for 8-MOP in complex with G3 and G4 dendrimer in relation to standard 8-MOP solution.

### 3.3.1.3 Dendrimers in Oral Drug Delivery

Oral drug-delivery system has been the dominant route for many years because of its significant advantages. It is by far the most convenient administration route with good patient compliance. Along with these benefits, there are also some defects of oral delivery route like low solubility in aqueous solutions and low penetration across intestinal membranes [41]. An ideal macromolecular carrier for orally administrated drugs should have the ability to protect the drugs from degrading. They might reduce nonspecific interactions with food proteins and allow enhanced absorption across the intestinal epithelium [42]. Duncan et al. [43] systematically investigated the effect of dendrimer size, charge, and concentration on uptake by the adult rat intestine and studied the absorption mechanisms of dendrimers in intestine tissues so as to develop PAMAM dendrimers as potential oral drug carriers. It was suggested that dendrimer size was a key factor on determining overall uptake [44]. Oral drug delivery studies using the human colon adeno carcinoma cell line (Caco-2) have indicated that low-generation PAMAM dendrimer across cell membranes, presumably through a combination of processes, i.e. paracellular transport and adsorptive endocytosis. Remarkably, the P-Glyco protein (Pgp) efflux transporter does not appear to affect dendrimers, therefore drug dendrimer complexes are able to bypass the efflux transporter [45]. But with increase in the concentration and generation, there was increase in the cytotoxicity and permeation of dendrimers. Ke et al. [46] developed a drug–PAMAM complex for oral administration. Doxorubicin was loaded into PAMAM, the cellular uptake and pharmacokinetics of the doxorubicin–PAMAM complex was studied. As the results, the cellular uptake of doxorubicin in Caco-2 cells treated with the doxorubicin–PAMAM complex was increased significantly with an increase in concentration and time, as compared to that treated with free doxorubicin. And the transport efficiency of the doxorubicin–PAMAM complex from the mucosal side to the serosal side was 4–7 times higher than that of free doxorubicin in different segments of small intestines of rat. The doxorubicin–PAMAM complex led to the bioavailability that was more than 200-fold higher than that of free doxorubicin after oral administration. These results indicate that PAMAM dendrimer is a promising novel carrier to enhance the oral bioavailability of drug, especially for the P-glycoprotein (P-gp) substrates.

### 3.3.1.4.Dendrimers in Pulmonary Drug Delivery

The ability to deliver proteins and peptides to the systemic circulation by inhalation has contributed to a rise in the number of inhalation therapies under investigation. For most of these therapies, aerosols are designed to comprise small spherical droplets or particles suitable for particle penetration into the airways or lung periphery. Studies performed primarily with liquid aerosols have shown that these characteristics of inhaled aerosols lead to optimal therapeutic effect. Though still inefficient drug delivery can still arise, owing to excessive particle aggregation in an inhaler, deposition in the mouth and throat, and overly rapid particle removal from the lungs by mucocilliary or phagocytic clearance mechanisms. To address these problems, particle surface chemistry and surface roughness are traditionally manipulated [47].

During one study, efficacy of PAMAM dendrimers in enhancing pulmonary absorption of

Enoxaparin was studied by measuring plasma anti-factor (Xa) activity, and by observing

prevention efficacy of deep vein thrombosis in a rodent model. G2 and G3 generation positively

charged Poly (amidoamine) dendrimers increased the relative bioavailability of Enoxaparin by

40%, while G2.5 PAMAM half generation dendrimers, containing negatively charged carboxylic

groups had no effect. Formulations did not adversely affect mucociliary transport rate or

produce extensive damage to the lungs. So, the positively charged dendrimers are suitable

carrier for Enoxaparin pulmonary delivery [48]. The absorption-enhancing effects of poly

amidoamine (PAMAM) dendrimers with various generations i.e. G0–G3 and concentrations i.e.

0.1%–1.0% (w/v) on the pulmonary absorption of peptide and protein drugs were studied in

rats [49]. Insulin and calcitonin were chosen as models of peptide and protein drugs, and their

pulmonary absorption with or without PAMAM dendrimers was examined by in vivo pulmonary

absorption studies. PAMAM dendrimers significantly increased the pulmonary absorption of

insulin and calcitonin in rats, and their absorption-enhancing effects were generation

dependent. The adsorption-enhancing effects were increased with increase in generations. For

the same generation, the absorption-enhancing effects of PAMAM dendrimers were shown to

be concentration dependent. Dendrimers did not cause any membrane damage to the lung

tissues. So, dendrimers are promising polymers for pulmonary drug delivery.

### 3.2.1.5.Dendrimers in Controlled Release Drug Delivery

Controlled release drug delivery is a new way to treat illnesses. The term controlled release

refers to the ability of a drug delivery system to release a drug over an extended period of time at a controlled rate. It generally involves implanting an engineered polymer directly into the organ or system that is affected by a disease. Since the polymer is implanted directly into the tissues affected by disease, the side-effects are often small compared to systemic drug delivery. Dendrimers offer advantages including a lower polydispersity index, multiple sites of attachment, and a controllable, well-defined size and structure that can be easily modified to change the chemical properties of the system [50]. In addition, macromolecules such as dendrimers have an enhanced permeability and retention effect that allows them to target tumor cells more effectively than small molecules [51]. Liu et al. [52, 53] have prepared poly (aryl-ether) dendrimers containing dual functionality on the surface. One is used to attach poly (ethylene glycol) (PEG) units on the surface to improve water solubility and the other one is utilized to attach hydrophobic drug molecules. They have also synthesized a series of dendritic uni-molecular micelles with a hydrophobic polyether core surrounded by a hydrophilic PEG shell for drug encapsulation. A third-generation micelle with indomethacin entrapped as model drug gives slow and sustained in vitro release, as compared to cellulose membrane control [54]. Poly (ethyleneglycol) PEG-2000 was conjugated to G3 Poly (amidoamine) (PAMAM) with varying degree of substitution. Methotrexate drug was encapsulated to the prepared conjugates and investigated for drug release in a dialysis bag. The results found that PEG dendrimers conjugated with encapsulated drug and sustained release of methotrexate as compare to no encapsulated drug. Asthana et al. [55] achieved controlled release of the Flurbiprofen by formation of complex with amine terminated G4 PAMAM dendrimers. Prepared dendrimer complexes observed that loaded drug displayed initial rapid release (more that 40% till 3rd hour) followed by slow release. Pharmacodynamic study was performed using carrageenan induced pawedema model, revealed 75% inhibition at 4th hour that was maintained above 50% till 8th hour. The dendritic formulation showed 2-fold and 3-foldincrease in mean residence time and terminal half-life, respectively, as compared to free drugs. The results show potential of dendrimers in controlled release drug delivery.

### 3.3.2. Dendrimers in Cancer Research/ Targeted Drug Delivery

The application of drug carrier systems for targeting tumor cells has gained importance as an alternative approach for treating cancer and offers both increased therapeutic index and decreased drug resistance. Thereby increasing efficacy and 3reducing side effects of chemotherapy. An effective targeting drug-delivery system requires a base that is uniform and able to couple multiple components such as targeting molecule, drug and cancer imaging agent [56]. Dendrimers have ideal properties which are useful in targeted drug-delivery system. One of the most effective cell-specific targeting agents delivered by dendrimers is folic acid. Membrane associated high-affinity folate receptors are folate-binding proteins that are over expressed on the surface of different types of cancer cells e.g. ovarian. Choi et al. [57] produce dendrimers conjugated to different biofunctional moieties like fluorescein and folic acid, and then link them together using complementary DNA oligonucleotides to produce clustered molecules that cancer cells that overexpress the high affinity folate receptor. These conjugates were injected i.e. into immuno deficient mice bearing human KB tumors that overexpress the folic acid receptor. These folate-conjugated nanoparticles concentrated in the tumor and liver tissue over 4 days after administration. Targeting methotrexate increased its antitumor activity and markedly decreased its toxicity, allowing therapeutic responses which are not possible with a free drug. Patri et al. [58] have investigated that complexing a drug with dendrimer as an inclusion complex improves its solubility in water, a cleavable, while covalently linked dendrimer conjugate is better for targeted drug delivery because it does not release the drug prematurely in biological conditions. They reported less cytotoxic effect with the covalently linked dendrimer. Sharma et al. [59] studied synthesis of a surface modified dendrimer for cancer targeted drug delivery system. For this, G4 PAMAM dendrimer 446 was conjugated with Gallic acid and characterized through UV, IR, $^1$H-NMR and mass spectroscopy. Cytotoxicity study of dendrimer conjugate was carried out against MCF-7 breast cancer cell line using MTT assay. The study revealed that the conjugate is active against MCF-7 cell line and might act synergistically with anti-cancer drug and gallic acid–dendrimer conjugate might be a promising nano-platform for cancer targeting and cancer diagnosis.

### 3.2.3. Dendrimer in Gene Delivery

Dendrimers have unique molecular architectures and properties that make them attractive materials for the development of nano-medicines. Key properties such as defined architecture and a high ratio of multivalent surface moieties to molecular volume also make these nanoscaled materials highly interesting for the development of synthetic (non-viral) vectors for therapeutic nucleic acids [60]. Besides of that some research recently indicated that dendrimer based gene delivery system also have significant potential in clinical trials. Kukowska-Latallo et al. [61] reported that intravenous administration of G9 Poly(amidoamine) (PAMAM) dendrimer-complexed pCF1CAT plasmid could result in high levelof gene expression in the lung tissues of rats. It enhances the transfection efficiency and expression pattern of dendrimers. Joester et al. [62] synthesized amphiphilic dendrimers having a rigid diphenylethyne core featured a variety of geometries and substitution patterns, all of which showed high transfection activity. The hydrophobic parameters influenced the DNA binding and transport more strongly than anticipated, exhibiting lower toxicity. In contrast to cationic dendrimers, these dendrimers did not have any size limitation for transfection. In another study; Takahashi et al. [63] synthesized amphiphilic, PAMAM dendrimers of generations 1 to 4, and utilizing di-n-dodecylamine as the core. These complexes with DNA and, in case of the G 2–4 dendrimers, were able to cross cell membranes and efficiently deliver DNA. Huang et al. [64] conjugated ligand Transferrin with PAMAM dendrimer using bifunctional polyethylene glycol. This vector showed 2.25 fold increases in gene transfection compared with PAMAM and PAMAM-PEG in vivo. Yu et al. [65] introduced histidine residues into L-arginine grafted PAMAM G4 dendrimers to enhance proton buffering capacity and evaluated the physicochemical characteristics and transfection efficacies in vitro. The results showed that the synthesized PAMAM G4 derivatives effectively delivered p-DNA (plasmid DNA) inside cells and the transfection level improved considerably as the number of histidine residues increased.

### 3.2.4. Dendrimers in Catalysis

The combination of high surface area and high solubility makes dendrimer useful as nanoscale catalysts [66]. They combine the advantages of both homogenous and heterogeneous catalysts. Homogenous catalysts are effective due to a good accessibility of active sites but they are often difficult to separate from the reaction stream. Heterogeneous catalysts are easy to separate from the reaction mixture but the kinetics of the reaction is limited mass transport. Dendrimers have a multifunctional surface and all catalytic sites are always exposed towards the reaction mixture. They can be recovered from the reaction mixture by easy ultra-filtration methods. The first example of a catalytic silane dendrimer was described by the group of Van Koten [67].

Bhyrappa et al. [68] developed a series of oxidatively robust poly(phenylesters) dendrimers were through a convergent synthesis. Significantly greater regioselectivity is observed with the dendrimer metalloporphyrins, relative to the corresponding parent 5,10,15,20-tetraphenylporphyrinato manganese (III) cation. In metallodendrimer, heterogeneous catalysis are a nickel-containing dendrimer are also reported active in the Kharasch Addition [69], palladium-containing dendrimers active in ethylene polymerization [70] and in the Heck Reaction (Smith, 2004). Karakhanov et al. [71] developed Bimetallic Cu (II) and Pd (II) metal complexes with nitrile-based dendrimers demonstrated high activity in Wacker Oxidation of terminal alkenes along with good selectivity for methylketone formation and same group has developed new heterogeneous catalysts based on Pd nanoparticles and cross-linked poly(propylene-imine) and poly(amidoamine) dendrimers were prepared and examined for selective hydrogenation of unsaturated compounds.

Rajesh Krishnan et al. [72] used poly (amidoamide) dendrimers as organo-catalysts for "Knoevenagel" and "Mannich" reactions in water. Knoevenagel Condensation between carbonyl compounds and active methylene compounds as well as three component Mannich Reaction between aldehydes, ketones and amines proceeded smoothly in water with good to excellent yield and high selectivity in the presence of zero and first generation poly (amidoamine)dendrimer.

### 3.2.5. Dendrimer as Membranes

Dendrimer with high degree of branching units, high density of surface functional groups, nano-scaled size, well-defined molecular weight and low-dispersity are suitable as membranes. Proton exchange membrane fuel cell (PEMFC) is believed to be the best type of fuel cell as a new clean and high efficient power, which will eventually replace the gasoline and diesel internal combustion engines. The function of the proton exchange membrane (PEM) is use to conduct the protons and separate the catalyst. Lee et al. [73] employed PAMAM dendrimers as components of PEM for fuel cells. Compared to the traditional "Nafion117", the membrane containing PAMAM dendrimers has higher proton conductivity but lower fuel permeability even under low humidity condition and or at high temperatures.

Bipolar membrane is a type of composition membrane, which contains a cation-exchanging layer, an anion exchanging layer and an interfacial layer. The novel property of a bipolar membrane is that the water molecules can be dissociated efficiently into the hydrogen ions and hydroxyl ions under reverse potential bias. To improve the water dissociation ability of a bipolar membrane, PAMAM dendrimers were used as catalysts of the water dissociation process in the intermediate layer of a bipolar membrane by Fu et al. [74]. They prepared the new bipolar membrane by immersing the heterogeneous anion exchanging membrane into Poly (amidoamine) (PAMAM) dendrimer aqueous solutions and casting the N,N-dimethylformamide (DMF) solution of sulphonated poly(phenylene oxide) (SPPO) onto the dendrimer treated anion exchanging membrane.

Sarkar et al. [75] reported first use of dendrimer in the modification of reverse osmosis (RO) membranes. The effects of dendrimer surface coatings on the advancing water contact angle i.e., coatings' hydrophilicity, permeate flux and % salt rejection of commercial polyamide membranes were studied. The membranes were coated by in situ crosslinking of amine-functional polyamidoamine (PAMAM) dendrimers and PAMAM–polyethylene glycol (PAMAM–PEG) multi-arm stars with difunctional PEG crosslinkers. The resulting coatings significantly reduced contact angles of membrane surfaces without affecting their % salt rejection and only moderately reducing their permeate fluxes. Lower contact angles indicated more hydrophilic membranes with the potential for increased resistance to fouling b hydrophobic foulants, such as biofoulants and organic pollutants.

### 3.2.6. Dendrimers as MRI Contrast Agents

Dendrimer based metal chelates act as a magnetic resonance imaging contrast agent.Dendrimers are highly suited and used asimage contrast media because of their properties. Many tests carried on dendrimershave shown that dendrimers are stronger contrast agent than conventional ones. They can improve visualisation of vascular structurein magnetic resonance angiography (MRA) of the body. Moreover, the sixth generationpolygadolinium dendrimer displayed a prolonged enhancement with a half-life of 200min compared to 24 min for monovalent gadolinium agent. This prolongedenhancement time is extremely useful for3Dtime-of-flight MR angiography [76]. In the recent study, it was found that the molecular size of adendrimer-based MRI agent altered the routeof excretion. Contrast agents havingmolecular weight less than 60 kDa were excreted through kidney being potentially suitable as functional renal contrast agents. Larger sized and hydrophilic contrast agents were found better for use as blood pool contrast agent. Larger hydrophilic agents were useful for lymphatic imaging. Finally, these dendrimer based MRI agents were recognised by the pharmaceutical industry which results in various commercial developments.

### 3.2.7. Dendrimers used for enhancing the solubility

PAMAM dendrimers are expected to have potential applications in enhancing the solubility for drug delivery systems [77, 78]. Dendrimers have hydrophilic exteriors and hydrophilic interiors, which are responsible for its unimolecular micelle nature. They form covalent as well as non-covalent complexes with drug molecules and hydrophobes, which are responsible for its solubilisation behaviour [79]. Dendrimers that are soluble in water are capable of binding and solubilising small acidic hydrophobic molecule with antifungal or antibacterial activities. Dendrimer possess unimolecular micelle and do not possess a critical micelle concentration. These characteristic offers the opportunity to soluble poorly soluble drugs by encapsulating them within the dendritic structure [79]. Dendrimer based carriers' offers the opportunity to enhance the oral bioavailability of problematicdrugs. Thus, dendrimer nanocarriers offer thepotential to enhance the bioavailability of drugs that are poorly soluble and/or substrates for efflux transporters.

### 3.2.8. Dendrimers for Additives Printing Inks and Paints

Dendrimers can be used in toners material with additives which require less material thantheir liquid counterparts. Xerox Corp. Patented a dry toner compound dendrimers as chargeenhancing species in the form of an additive [80]. Using additives in printing inks, dendriticpolymers ensure uniform adhesion of ink to polar and non-polar foils. Here, first the hyperbranched compounds attach themselves to the pigment particles and there are still large numbers of functional groups remaining to give adhesion to the surface of the foils. Dendritic polymers used in polyurethanepaints impart surface hardness, scratch resistance, chemical resistance, light fastness, weathering resistance as well as high gloss, because of which they are used in furniture and automotive industries. Use of Dendrimer additives in the composition of the invention is effective for altering the surface characterization of thermo plastic resin after moulding. One of example for this is polycarbonates, which are widely used as an engineering thermoplastic for providing a unique combination of toughness, stiffness, high softening

temperature                                    and                                    processibility.

### 3.2.9. Dendrimers as Light Harvesting Materials

A significant research has been of interest for designing molecules with controlled motion of

charges. The use of Dendrimers is because of its multiple functionality and structural features.

Moving from the periphery to the core, the functional groups decreases; which render

dendrimers in light harvesting. Most of the literature report shows direction towards energy

funnelling from the chromophore in the periphery to another chromophore at the core [81]. A

study on π-conjugated dendrimers family based on truxene and thienylethynylene

weresynthesised. These synthesised dendrimers show intrinsic energy gradient from periphery

to the core along with broad absorption in the UV-vis range and proficient energy transfer to

the lower energy centre. Hence, they are highly potential as light harvesting materials.

### 3.2.10.                    Dendrimers                    as                    Biomimics

Dendrimers having their well-defined macromolecular dimensions and compartmentalised

structure are ideal mimics for a wide variety of biomolecules. The commercially available

dendrimers provide possibility to create micro environments. PAMAM dendrimers with their

network consisting of numerous mixed tertiary amines. Dendrimers have ability to expose the

multivalent surface for increased binding of biomolecules. Also, dendrimers have ability to

create a micro environment inside the dendrimer, which makes artificial catalytic sites or

cavities possessing different properties for construction of enzyme mimics. Dendrimer

molecules are characterized by zones of different density, depending upon the rigidity or the

conformational mobility of their scaffold; they combine dense and less dense areas. They are flexible and have cavities to accommodate solvent to act as host compounds for guest substance. By using dendrimers more favourable qualities compared to naturally occurring proteins canbe obtained. More densely packed structure compared to the natural proteins, for example certain peptide based dendrimer system show a significant increased resistance towards proteases [82]. The dendrimer is also used as a building block to mimic a non-globular collagen structure, showing that dendrimers, although being mostly globular shaped, may be used as mimics of non-globular structures. Dendrimers may also mimic numerous protein – based receptors utilised in nature for specific biological recognition. Glycomometics are synthesized analogous carbohydrate whose structure has been simplified and modified, and is an active ingredient, which can be used for treatment of chronic inflammatory ailment such as rheumatism, dermatitis and soriasis. (According to Diederich et al) Dendritic porphyrin-metal complexes consist of flexible dendritic poly (ether amide) units [83]. Study of first and second generations of this dendrimer revealed that the reductionpotential is shifted towards positive values, than sufficient shielding is obtained.

### 3.2.11. Dendrimers as Separating Agents

A study of variety of compounds synthesized to determine suitability for enhancing boron rejection by reverse osmosis and nano-filtration membrane to separate born from sea water has been developed. For separation, compound must have amphiphile chemical structure and form micelle in aqueous solution. As a new compound dendrimers with a high density of functional moiety, is able to form micelle structure which can be easily separated and recovered by ultrafiltration membrane. These micelles provide high functional density at the surfaceof the particle, high surface area and ease of separation for isolation and regeneration of the compound. It was found that unmodified commercial dendrimeric compounds containing amine and hydroxyl groups are generally more effective for boron absorption. Polyamidoamine (PAMAM) dendrimers are used as chelating agents for the removal of certain metal ions from waste water [84] and from contaminated soil [85].Other modified chelating PAMAM and poly (propyleneimine) dendrimer are also reported to be good ligands for a various hard metal cations [86, 87] or can be described as "nanosponges" for the removal of Polycyclic aromatic hydrocarbons [88] and other particles [89, 90]. Patel et al. [91] utilized hydroxyl terminated triazine based dendrimers to remove Copper, Zinc and Nickel ions from water.

## References

1. E. Bhuleier, W. Wehner, F. Vogtle. Synthesis. 155**(1978)**.

2. R. Moors, F. Vögtle, Chem. Ber. **126**, 2133**(1993)**.

3. J. C. Hummelen, J. L. J. Van Dongen, E. W. Meijer, Chem. Eur. J. **3**,1489**(1997)**.

4.D. A. Tomalia, H. Baker, J. Dewald, M. Hall, G. Kallos, S. Martin, J. Roeck, J. Ryder, P. Smith; Polymer J., 1985, **17**, 117**(1986)**.

5. I. J. Majoros, L. Piechler, D. A. Tomalia, J. R. Baker Jr., "Synthesis and Characterization of Novel POPAM-PAMAM (POMAM) Hybrid Dendrimers as a Building Block in Nanotechnology."http://www.forsight.org/conferences/ MNT8/abstract/Baker/index.html.

6. P.R. Dvornic, A.M. de Leuze-Jallouli, M. J.Owen, S.V. Perz, Macromolecules. **33**, 53**(2000)**.

7. K. Lorenz, D. Hölter, B. Stühn, R. Mülhaupt, H. Frey. Adv. Mater. **8**,414**(1996)**.

8. N. Boiko, X. Zhu, A. Bobrovsky, V. Shibaev. Chem. Mater. **13**, 1447**(2001)**.

9. T.A. Betley, J.A. Hessler, A. Mecke, M.M. Banaszak Holl, B.G. Orr, S. Uppuluri, D. A. Tomalia, J.R. Baker Jr. Langmuir. **18**, 3127**(2002)**.

10. A. Ritzén, T. Frejd, Chem. Commun. 207**(1999)**.

11. N. K. Jain, A.J. Khopade. Dendrimers as potential delivery systems for bioactives. In: Jain, N.K. (Ed.), "Advances in controlled and novel drug delivery." CBS Publishers & Distributors, New Delhi, , 361**(2001)**.

12. M. Colinger. Curr. Opin. Chem. Biol. **6**, 742**(2002)**.

13. B. Qualmann, M. M. Kessels, H.-J. Musiol, W. D. Sierralta, P. W. Jungblut, L. Moroder, Angew. Chem. **108**, 970**(1996)**.

14. R. G. Denkewalter, J. Kolc, W. J. Lukasavage; Preparation of lysine based macromolecular highly branched compound, U.S. Patent No. 4,360,646 **(1979).**

15.R. G. Denkewalter, J. Kolc, W. J. Lukasavage; Macromolecular highly branched homogeneous compound based on lysine units, U.S. Patent No. 4,289,872 **(1981).**

16. R. G. Denkewalter, J. Kolc, W. J. Lukasavage; Macromolecular highly branched homogeneous compound, U.S. Patent No. 4,410,688 **(1983).**

17. N. Röckendorf, T. K. Lindhorst, Top. Curr. Chem. (Volume Eds. F. Vögtle,C. A. Schalley) **217**, 201**(2002)**.

18. R. Roy, D. Zanini, J. Meunier, A. Romanowska, J. Chem. Soc., Chem. Commun., 1869**(1993)**.

19. R. Roy, Polymer News, **21**, 226**(1996)**.

20. F. Bambino, R. T. Brownlee, F. C. Chiu, Tetrahedron Lett. **35**, 4619 **(1994)**.

21. P. R. Ashton, S. E. Boyd, C. L. Brown, N. Jayaraman, S. A. Nepogodiev, J. F. Stoddart, Chem. Eur. J. **2**, 1115 **(1996)**.

22. K. Sadalapure, T. K. Lindhorst, Angew. Chem. **112**, 2066 **(2000)**.

23. M. Dubber, T. K. Lindhorst, Chem. Commun. 1265**(1998)**.

24. M.Ballauff, C.N. Likos; Angew. Chem. Int. Ed., **43(23)**, 2998 **(2004)**.

25. E.W.Meijer, M.W.P.L. Baars; Topics in Current Chemistry, **210**, 131 **(2000)**.

26. D. Gajjar, R. Patel, P.M. Patel, Macromolecules: An Indian Journal, **10(1)**, 37, **(2014)**.

27. R.Gaudana, J. Jwala, S.H.S. Boddu, A.K. Mitra. Pharm.Res., **26(5)**, 1197 **(2008)**.

28. A.Kumar, R.Malviya, P.K. Sharma; Eur. J. Applied Sci., **3(3)**, 86 **(2011)**.

29. A.Quintana, E.Raczka, L.Piehler, I.Lee, A. Myc, I.Majoros,A.K.Patri,T.Thomas, J.Mule, J.R.BakerJr.; Pharm.Res., **19**, 1310 **(2002)**.

30. H.R.Ihre, O.L.Padilla De Jesus, F.C. Szoka Jr, J.M.J.Frechet; Bioconjug.Chem., **13**, 443 **(2002)**.

31. S.K.Sahoo, F.Dilnawaz, S. Krishnakumar. Drug Discov Today, **13**, 144 **(2008)**.

32. T.F.Vandamme, L.Brobeck; J.Control. Rel., **102**, 23 **(2005)**.

33. G.T.Tolia, H.H.Choi, F. Ahsan; Pharm. Technol., **32(11)**, 88 **(2008)**.

34. G.Spataro, F.Malecaze, C.O.Turrin, V. Soler, C.Duhayon, P.Elena, J.P.Majoral,A.M.Caminade;Eur.J.Med.Chem., **45(1)**, 326 **(2010)**.

35. W.Yao, K.Sun, H.Mu, N.Liang, Y.Liu, C. Yao, R.Liang,A.Wang;DrugDevelop.Ind.Pharm., **36(9)**,1027 **(2010)**.

36. M.R.Prausnitz, R. Langer; Nature Biotechnol.,**26**,1261 **(2008)**.

37. Z.X.Wang, Y. Itoh, Y. Hosaka, I. Kobayashi, Y.Nakano, I.Maeda, F.Umeda, J. Yamakawa, M.Kawase, K.Yag; J.Biosci.Bioengg.,**95(5)**, 541 **(2003)**.

38. C.Yiyun, M.Na, X.Tongwen, F. Rongqiang, W.Xueyuan,W.Xiaomin,W.Longping; J.Pharm.Sci.,**96(3)**, 595 **(2007)**.

39. A.S.Chauhan, S.Sridevi, K.B.Chalasani,A.K. Jain, S.K.Jain, N.K.Jain, P.V.Diwan; J.Control. Rel., **90(3)**, 335 **(2003)**.

40. K.Borowska, S.Woùowieca, A. Rubajb, K.Gùowniakc, E.Sieniawskac, S.Radejd; Inter.J.Pharm., **426(12)**, 280 **(2012)**.

41. N.Csaba, M.Garcia-Fuentes, M.J. Alonso; Exp.Opin.Drug Deliv., **3(4)**, 463 **(2006)**.

42.C.Yiyun, M. Na, X. Tongwen, F. Rongqiang, W.Xueyuan,W.Xiaomin,W.Longping; J.Pharm. Sci.,**96(3)**, 595 **(2007)**.

43.R.Duncan, R.Wiwattanapatapee, B. Carreno- Gomez, N.Malik; Pharm.Res., **17(8)**, 991 **(2000)**.

44. A.T.Florence,T.Sakthivel, I.Toth; J.Control. Rel., **65,**253 **(2000)**.

45. A.D. Emanuele, A.R.Jevprasesphant, R.J. Penny, D.Attwood; J.Control.Rel., **95(3)**, 447 **(2004)**.

46. W.Ke, Y.Zhao, R.Huang, C.Jiang, R. Pei; J.Pharm.Sci., **97(6)**, 2208 **(2008)**.

47. D.A.Edwards, A.Ben-Jebria, R. Langer; J.Appl.Physiol., **85(2)**, 379 **(1998)**.

48. S.Bai, C.Thomas, F.Ahsan; J. Pharm. Sci., **96(8)**, 2090 **(2007)**.

49. Z.Dong, K.A.Hamid, Y.Gao, Y.Lin, H.Katsumi,T.Sakane,A.Yamamoto; J.Pharm.Sci., **100(5)**, 1866

50. M.Liu, J.M.J.Fréchet; Pharm. Sci. Technol. Today, **2(10)**, 393 **(1999)**.

51. H.Maeda, J.Fang, T.Inutsuka, Y. Kitamoto; Int.Immunopharmacol.,**3(3)**, 319 **(2003)**.

52. M.Liu,K.Kono, J.M.J.Fréchet; J.Polym.Sci. Part A: Polym.Chem., **37(17)**, 3492 **(1999)**.

53. M.Liu, K.Kono, J.M.J.Fréchet; J.Control. Rel., **65**, 121 **(2000)**.

54. A.K.Patri, I.J.Mojoros, J.R.Baker Jr.;Curr.Opin.Chem.Biol., **6**, 466 **(2002)**.

55. A.Asthana, A.A.Chauhan, P.V.Diwan, N.K. Jain; AAPS Pharm.Sci.Tech, **6**, E536 **(2005)**.

56. T.P.Thomas, A.K.Patri, A.Myc, M.T. Myaing, J.Y.Ye, B.Morris, J.R.Baker Jr.; Biomacromole., **5(6)**, 2269 **(2004)**.

57. Y.Choi,T.Thomas,A.Kotlyar,M.T.Islam, J.R.BakerJr.; Chem.Biol., **12(1)**, 35 **(2005)**.

58. A.K.Patri, J.F.Kukowska-Latallo, J.R. Baker Jr.; Adv.Drug Deliv.Rev., **57**, 2203 **(2005)**.

59. A.Sharma, S.P.Gautam, A.K. Gupta; Bioorg.Med.Chem., **19(11)**, 3341 **(2011)**.

60. C.Dufes, I.F.Uchegbu, A.G.Schatzlein; Adv.DrugDelivery Rev., **57**, 2177 **(2005)**.

61. J.F.Kukowska-Latallo, C.Chen, E. Raczka, A.Qunintana, M.Rymaszewski, J.R. Baker; Hum.Gene.Ther.,**11**, 1385 **(2000)**.

62. D.Joester, M.Losson, R.Pugin, H. Heinzelmann, E.Walter, H.P.Merkle, F. Diederich; Angew.Chem.Int.Ed., **42**, 1486 **(2003)**.

63. T.Takahashi, K.Kono, T.Itoh, N.Emi, T. Takagishi; Bioconjug.Chem., **14**, 764 **(2003)**.

64. R.Q.Huang, Y.H.Qu, W.L.Ke, J.H.Zhu, Y.Y. Pei, C.Jiang; FASEB Journal, **21(4)**, 1117 **(2007)**.

65.G.S.Yu, Y.M.Bae, H.Choi, B.Kong, I.S. Choi, J.S.Choi; Bioconjug.Chem., **22**, 1046 **(2011)**.

66. D.A.Tomalia, P.R.Dvornic; Nature, **372(6507)**, 617 **(1994)**.

67. J.W.J.Knapen, A.W.Van der Made, J.C.de Wilde,P.W.N.M.Van Leeuwen,

P.Wijkens,D.M.Grove,G.van Koten; Nature, 372**(6507)**, 659 **(1994)**.

68. P.Bhyrappa, J.K.Young, J.S.Moore, K.S.Suslick; J.Am.Chem.Soc., **118(24)**, 5708 **(1996)**.

69. G.Smith, R.Chen, S.Mapolie; J.Org.Mett. Chem., **673(1-2)**, 111 **(2003)**.

70. G.Smith, S.F.Mapolie; J. Mol. Cat.A: Chem., **213(2)**, 187 **(2004)**.

71. E.A.Karakhanov, A.L.Maximov, V.A. Skorkin, A.V.Zolotukhina,A.S.Smerdov,A.Y.Tereshchenko;Pure.Appl.Chem., **81(11)**, 2013 **(2009)**.

72. G.Rajesh Krishnan, J. Thomas, K. Sreekumar; Arkivoc, **10**, 106 **(2009)**.

73. J.H.Lee,H.S.Shin,H.W.Rhee,Y.T.Kim,M.K.Song,M.S.Kim; U.S.Patent No. 2006116479.

74. R.Q.Fu, T.W.Xu, Y.Y.Cheng,W.H.Yang, Z.X.Pan;J.Membrane.Sci., **240**, 141 **(2004)**.

75. A.Sarkar, P.I.Carver, T.Zhang, A.Merrington,K.J.Bruza, J.L.Rousseau, S.E.Keinath,P.R.Dvornic; Journal of Membrane Science, **349(1-2)**, 421 **(2010)**.

76. N.K. Jain. Advances in Controlled and Novel Drug Delivery'CBS Publishers &Distributors Pvt.Ltd.Reprint, 361 **(2010)**.

77. D.A. Tomalia, H. Baker, J.R. Dewald, M.Hall, G. Kallos, S. Martin, J. Roeck, J. Ryder P. Smith. Dendrimers II: Architecture,nanostructure and supramolecularchemistry, Macromolecules, **19**, 2466,**(1986)**.

78. P.E. Froehling, Dendrimers and dyes - a review, Dyes and pigments, **48**, 187,**(2001)**.

79. N.K.Jain, U .Gupta, Expert Opin. Drug Metab. Toxicol, **8**, 1035 **(2008)**.

80. F.M. Winnick, J.M. Duff, G. G. Sacripante, A. R.Davidson (Xerox Corp.), USA  5256516 A 931026, **(1993)**; Chem. Abstr, 120, 90707i,**(1994)**.

81. A. Nantalaksakul, D. R. Reddy, T.-S.Ahn,R.-A. Kaysi, C. J. Bardeen, S. ThayumanavanOrg.Lett., **8,** 2981**(2006)**.

82. H. Sashiwa, H. Yajima, S. Aiba, Biomacromolecules, **4**, 1244**(2003)**.

83. L. Bracci, C. Falciani, B. Lelli, L. Lozzi, Y. Runci, A. Pini, M.G. De Montis, A. Tagliamonte, P. Neri, J. Biol. Chem, **278**, 46590, **(2003)**.

84. M. Diallo, S. Christie, P. Swaminathan, J.Johnson, W. Goddard.Environmental Science and Technology, **39(5)**, 1366 **(2005)**.

85. Y-H Xu,D-Y. Zhao.Environ. Sci. Technol, **39**, 2369**(2005)**.

86. S. M. Cohen, S. Petoud, K. N. Raymond.Chem. Eur. J, **7(1)**, 272**(2001)**.

87. A. Rether, M. Schuster, Reactive and Functional Polymers, **57**, 13, **(2003)**.

88. M. Arkas, D.Tsiourvas,C.M. Paleos. , Chem. Mater, **15**, 2844**(2003)**.

89. G.Pistilis, A. Malliaris.  Langmuir, **18**, 246**(2002)**.

90. H.N. Patel, P.M. Patel. Int. J. Pharma. Biosci. **4(2)**, 454 **(2013)**.

91. D. Gajjar, R. Patel, H. Patel, P. M. Patel. Chem. Sci. Trans. **(2014)**, In press,

DOI:10.7598/cst2014.834.

www.ingramcontent.com/pod-product-compliance
Lightning Source LLC
Chambersburg PA
CBHW020359290526
45785CB00005B/2355